NGOs in India

By examining how NGOs operate in southern India in the early 2000s, this book discusses the challenges faced by small, local NGOs in the uncertain times of changing aid dynamics. The key findings focus on what empowerment means for Indian women, and how NGO accountability to these women is an important part of the empowerment being realized.

The notion of community empowerment, in which the 'solidarity' of a group can be a path to individual empowerment, is discussed, as well as analysing how empowerment can be a useful concept in development. Based on case studies of 15 NGOs as well as in-depth interviews with 80 women's self-help groups, the book highlights the key features of effective empowerment programmes. The author uses innovative statistical analysis tools to show how a key factor in empowerment of marginalized women is the accountability relationship between themselves and the supporting NGO. The book goes on to discuss the ways that NGOs can work with communities in the future, and recognizes the limitations of a donor-centric accountability framework. It provides a useful contribution to studies on South Asia as well as Gender and Development Studies.

Patrick Kilby is a political scientist with the School of Archaeology and Anthropology in the College of Arts and Social Sciences at the Australian National University. His research interests include NGOs, poverty and women's empowerment.

Routledge contemporary South Asia series

NGOs in India

The challenges of women's empowerment and accountability

Patrick Kilby

Routledge
Taylor & Francis Group

LONDON AND NEW YORK

First published 2011
by Routledge
2 Park Square, Milton Park, Abingdon, Oxon OX14 4RN

Simultaneously published in the USA and Canada
by Routledge
711 Third Avenue, New York, NY 10017

Routledge is an imprint of the Taylor & Francis Group, an informa business

First issued in paperback 2012

© 2011 Patrick Kilby

Typeset in Times New Roman by Integra Software Services Pvt. Ltd, Pondicherry, India

British Library Cataloguing in Publication Data
A catalogue record for this book is available from the British Library

Library of Congress Cataloging in Publication Data
Kilby, Patrick.
NGOs in India : the challenges of women's empowerment and accountability / Patrick Kilby.
p.cm – (Routledge contemporary south asia series)
Includes bibliographical references and index.
1. Women in development – India. 2. Community development – India.
3. Non-governmental organizations – India. I. Title
HQ1240.5.I4K55 2010
305.48'969420954091724 – dc22
2010011863

ISBN 978–0–415–54430–6 (hbk)
ISBN 978–0–203–84272–0 (ebk)
ISBN 978–0–415–53367–6 (pbk)

Contents

Illustrations

Figures

Tables

Map

Acknowledgements

This book has provided me with an opportunity to repay those who have facilitated my work in development over the past 30 years and thank them for the pleasure this work has provided me. It has also enabled me to both satisfy and stimulate my questioning on how working in development can make a difference. But, most importantly, I am humbled by the strength of the Indian women, living in harsh circumstances, who gave up their precious free time to talk to me, a foreigner. Their courage and matter-of-fact approach to their lives is a source of inspiration. It is these many hundreds of women to whom I am most grateful.

I am also indebted to the staff and leadership of the 15 NGOs who also gave their time to talk so frankly about the dilemmas they face in their day-to-day work and provided so much of the intellectual input and ideas that drive this book. Likewise I am grateful to Oxfam Australia and the other affiliates of Oxfam International who facilitated my interaction with so many local NGOs, most of whom were their local partners.

Finally, special thanks go to Joyce Wu, my wife, friend and colleague, who is a lifelong inspiration to me, and offered much love and support in the writing of this book. She also generously made the time to read the later drafts of the book and offered important insights and suggestions, as well as a sharp proofreader's eye.

Permissions

Table 1 and Figure 2 are reprinted from Kilby, P. (2006) 'Accountability for empowerment: dilemmas facing non governmental organizations', *World Development*, 34(6): 951–963; with permission from Elsevier.

Glossary

balwadi	a pre-school
BGSS	Bharatiya Grameena Seva Sangh
BPL	Below Poverty Line: a category that triggers welfare subsidies
CAPART	Council for Advancement of People's Action and Rural Technology
Chinyard	Chaitanya Institute for Youth and Rural Development
Collector	Most senior district official: is appointed by Central Government
CSWB	Central Social Welfare Board
crore	Ten million rupees ($USD200,000)
CRY Foundation	Child Rights and You
dalits	literally translates as 'oppressed': the lowest grouping in the Indian caste system, formerly known as 'untouchables'
FCRA	Foreign Contributions Regulation Act
gram panchayat	Village Council
gram sabha	Village meeting: they elect the *gram panchayat*
Grama Vikas	Literally means 'village development'; often used as an NGO name
hindutva	a movement advocating Hindu nationalism
IDS	International Development Service
Jagruti	Literally means 'awakening' and the name of an NGO
KIDS	Karnataka Integrated Development Service
KKPKP	Kagad Kach Patra Kashtakari Panchayat (The Association of Wastepickers in the city)
MYRADA	formerly Mysore Relief and Development Association
NABARD	National Bank for Agriculture and Rural Development
Prakruthi	Literally means 'balance in mind and body'; is the name of an NGO
PREM	People's Rural Education Movement
NGO	Non-Governmental Organization
RORES	Reorganisation of Rural Economy and Society
sarpanch	village head

SEWA	Self-employed Women's Association
SHG	Self-help Group
SIDBI	Small Industries Development Bank of India
SNDT	Shreemati Nathibai Damodar Thackersey (Women's University – in this book refers to the Centre for Adult and Continuing Education, Pune campus)
tribals	Refers to members of scheduled tribes, which is a minority category under the Indian Constitution
UNDP	United Nations Development Program
YUVA	Youth for Voluntary Action

Introduction

NGOs are seen to have a central role in development practice, but the question that remains unanswered, and probably never can be answered, is: what role (or roles) should this be? This is not a new question; ever since NGOs as institutional forms came to have a role in social development in the eighteenth and nineteenth centuries, governments have seen them as service providers, while the NGOs' supporters have seen them as advocates for social change. For example, William Wilberforce and the anti-slavery movement, and the host of other social service organizations he was associated with, were devoted to both social service and social change. Two hundred years later, little has changed, with the same old debates continuing as to what roles NGOs should have, and how they can be effective. This book proposes to move the debate forward by looking at the factors that make NGOs' work effective, and the issues that NGOs face in meeting these requirements. In this book I will look at local NGOs in southern India as a case study, as they are well established, have a strong social change focus mainly through women's empowerment programmes, and are undergoing rapid structural change as a result of India's rapidly growing economy and the related change in their funding sources.

Indian NGOs have been involved in development work of one sort or another for over 100 years and have been important in Indian government programmes, as well as being partners for international NGO (INGO) donors since the nation's independence in 1947. My own interest comes from my work with Oxfam Australia since the mid-1980s, when Indian NGOs were an important part of the rural and urban development scene, while at the same time being treated rather warily by the government at the time. As this was before the deregulation of the 1990s, it was a period when the Indian state was more pervasive in people's daily lives and NGOs were under some surveillance. Since then, NGOs have become mainstream actors in development with not only INGOs supporting them, but also bilateral, multilateral, and a broader range of Indian state agencies being involved in NGO programmes.

During the mid-1980s, while local Indian NGOs were involved in broader social justice programmes, at a local level NGO programmes focused on income generation and the like for marginalized groups, with an increasing focus on women. SEWA an NGO in Ahmedabad, for example, had been looking at gender justice issues as well as income generation programmes for women since the mid-1970s, and by the mid-1980s their model was being picked up by NGOs across India, and the idea of the 'empowerment of women' was gaining currency. By the mid-1990s women's empowerment was a part of the lexicon, and all NGOs felt they had to subscribe to it, often with little idea of what it meant. The 1990s was also a time when NGO effectiveness was being questioned, after the optimism of the 1980s regarding the value of NGO work, and INGOs in particular were undertaking more evaluations of themselves and their partners' work, to ensure quality, and to be able to assure both their public and government supporters that they were being effective.

The other debate in the mid-1990s was the focus on women's programmes and empowerment, and the important issue of gender implicit in these programmes. This was energized by the Beijing women's conference, and the move in the debates from women and development (WID) to gender and development (GAD). A key feature of most NGO work in India, and certainly in southern and western India since the mid-1980s, was that the work was with mainly with women and the self-help group programmes were targeting women. In the 1990s there was also a shift in focus from income generation programmes for women, which invariably meant the household production of high labour low value products, towards a self-help group model which focused on saving within a group and with those savings gaining access to additional credit, which was then meant to be invested in assets for income generation and the like. While this was an improvement on income generation per se, often the NGOs' focus was still on income generation from relatively low value products, while discouraging using the savings and credit from the groups for household consumption, even if consumption was for improved health and education.

Being involved in some of these debates through this time I became interested in the empowerment question, particularly in the self-help group and microfinance context. Empowerment seemed to be one of those terms used in development that are slowly washed and bleached of any real meaning, to become more of a soundbite than a meaningful objective. Even politicians now use it as an election catchphrase. At the same time it seemed that looking at empowerment and the factors that may affect it, in a more direct sense, might give some insight into the effectiveness of local NGOs in India, and touch on the general challenges they face as NGOs. These debates and questions resulted in my field studies with NGOs in Karnataka and Maharashtra in India in the early 2000s, which have led to this book. A problem with this type of research is that during the time it may take to process and publish findings the context may have changed. Sometimes this can be for the better, as discussed in Chapter 4 with the rapid advances made by the waste-picker union in the ten years since this study started, to protect their livelihoods and rights in the face of social and technical change. In other cases, as outlined in Chapter 3, a changing context can lead to challenges and changes in the way local NGOs operate as the traditional/INGO donors leave the prosperous southern Indian states, to be replaced by the more restrictive Indian Government funding. While the contexts have changed, the central findings about the relationship of empowerment and accountability are still a key issue, and one that provides challenges for the Indian NGOs as they adapt to the changing environment in which they operate.

This book is structured in three broad parts. The first part, Chapters 1 and 2, set out the historical context of NGO work in India, particularly its often fraught relationship with the state. It examines how NGOs operate in the Indian context of the early 2000s, with the emphasis on the self-help group (SHG) as an approach to development work. The SHGs had their origins in southern India in the late 1970s, and now the use of SHGs is the preferred approach by Government and NGOs alike in community development work. It is in these chapters that the concept of empowerment is introduced as a development approach, and why it is seen to be important in development work. Chapters 3 and 4 look at NGO case studies and the local contexts where they were working: Chapter 3 focuses on NGOs in two districts of Karnataka, while Chapter 4 focuses on one case study, that of the waste-picker programme supported by an NGO in Pune City, Maharashtra. Although the waste-picker programme is urban based, while the rest of the book deals with rural areas, it is an important case as it provides a contrast and highlights the components for an effective programme of empowerment of a very marginalized group. A number of the case studies look at what can be done with ambitious and flexible approaches that don't easily fit the conventional project approach. Chapter 5 looks at the results of the field research from interviewing around 80 self help groups, and analysing what their members saw as empowering, while Chapter 6 looks at the factors that lead to strong empowerment outcomes; in particular, the vexed question of NGO accountability to the recipient groups they are working with, when facilitating empowerment programmes. Chapter 7 concludes with a discussion of the implications of these findings for NGO practice.

The analysis I have taken is a broad analysis with a large data set, rather than a few case studies, in order to get an indication of the breadth of changes across communities and groups rather than more in-depth ethnographic studies. I have tried, though, to capture where I can the insights from women of what change has meant for them. Likewise, even though the study is about women's empowerment and a gender analysis was undertaken, the limitations were that the strong patriarchal structure behind the marginalization of women in India is heavily gendered and that starts with household relations, which most NGOs avoid. The NGO programmes looked at did not seek to change these basic gender relations at the household level, and where they did change them it was marginal and hard to quantify (see Chapter 5). What they tended to do was to change women's access to a broader range of social and community domains which in many cases were highly gendered. The researcher's starting point was to look at these NGO programmes on their own terms and the changes that had occurred in women's lives as a result of these interventions.

This book highlights challenges faced by small local NGOs in southern India in the uncertain times of changing aid dynamics. The key findings are about what empowerment means for poor Indian women, and how accountability to these women's groups is an important part of women's empowerment being realized. The book concludes with some challenges for NGOs in how they work with communities, and how they may shift their concerns about accountability more to the people they serve than to the people who fund and regulate them.

1 Non-governmental organizations in India

Introduction

Non-governmental organizations (NGOs) in India have a rich and vibrant history, but one which has been characterized by a fluid relationship with the state and state instrumentalities. Over the past 150 years Indian governments, both colonial and postcolonial, have played a key role in shaping Indian NGOs, both in terms of how they function in society and their often fraught relationships with the state. Likewise, at key times in India's history, NGOs themselves have played a part in shaping the state. Generally, though, Indian NGOs are reluctant to admit that the state determines both the scope and nature of the work that they can undertake, and to some extent their structural forms – but like it or not, the relationship with the state is a defining feature of Indian NGOs. So who or what are these NGOs? Put simply, in India NGOs are those organizations that have some form of institutional base, are private, non-profit, self-governing, voluntary in nature, and registered with the government (Nandedkar 1987). The problem is that it is difficult to assess the range of NGOs in India that have NGO status from government, as there is no central mechanism to determine those that have been registered with the various local, state and national government instrumentalities (Sen 1993). This simple definition I have used hides a rather complex reality, which is the Indian NGO scene.

Estimates of the total number of voluntary organizations in India that are in some way or other recognized by the state, range from 1 to 2 million (Salamon and Anheier 1999). This rather indeterminate number of voluntary organizations working in India is in some way testament both to the difficulty in measuring numbers, and also to the importance that voluntary work is given in Indian society '… a timeless sphere conterminous with Indian civilization itself …' (Blamey and Pasha 1993: 14). This broad set of NGOs ranges from small village associations such as funeral societies and Parents and Citizens associations, all of which have some form of registration, to very large organizations that provide services to hundreds of thousands of people across several states. To narrow the scope of this vast field, this book is only concerned with those NGOs that work with poor and marginalized communities – 'development NGOs' of which there are around 80,000 (Salamon and Anheier 1999: 70). These numbers, like those for the broader NGO category, are still only estimates, as development NGOs are registered under Indian individual state legislation as either Trusts or Associations, and so these figures are notoriously hard to compile centrally with any accuracy. The only accurate number is the 32,144 NGOs which in 2006 were federally registered to receive foreign funds (Ministry of Home Affairs 2007), with a little over half of those registered actually receiving foreign funds in that year. So even with these figures, it is still hard to determine whether those that did not receive funding are still active in their host communities. They may well be active, but with reduced resources, given that many international NGO donors are reducing funding to many parts of India, a point that will be returned to in Chapter 3. There are of course the many NGOs that do development work, and do not wish to receive foreign funding but are supported by local resources, either voluntary or from Indian government instrumentalities (Jalali 2008).

The larger Indian development NGOs, had been mainly supported by foreign sources for their funding until the early 2000s, and received Rs7,877 crore or $US1.85b. in 2006 (Ministry of Home Affairs 2007: ii). In the past this accounted for over 90 per cent of the total formal funding of Indian NGOs involved in development work (Sen, S. 1999); however, from around 2005 Indian government funding started to displace international funding, particularly for the more secular NGOs in the more economically successful states in southern India.

> NGOs small and large that had relied on foreign funds have begun to actively explore ways to raise money from domestic sources … [with] many NGOs actively seeking and entering closer funding relationships with the state.
>
> (Kudva 2005: 248)

Again these statistics can hide a more complex reality, as there is a very high level of voluntary time given to NGOs, particularly the smaller ones that make up the bulk of the sector, and this has not been valued with any accuracy, but Tandon (2002) estimates the voluntary time together with private donations as being on the same scale as government and international funding combined. The high level of foreign funding to NGOs in the late 1990s and early 2000s reflected the popularity of NGOs as a conduit for foreign aid for poverty alleviation programmes, believing them to be more reliable and effective than government channels (Murthy and Rao 1997; Rajasekhar 1998). The limits placed by the Indian government on the number of bilateral donors it deals with saw all but six bilateral aid relationships terminated in 2003 (Times of India 2 June), provided new opportunities for both the Indian government and international NGOs, at least in the short term, to pick up the slack. This leads to the question of what makes the NGO sector such an important sector for donors and government funders alike?

What makes NGOs tick? Some theory

A recurring theme in modern development discourse is the role of NGOs in providing mechanisms for strengthening civil society for poor and marginalized communities (for example, see World Bank 1996). This process includes organizing and 'empowering' marginalized communities and, as such, is seen as an integral part of overcoming disadvantage and marginalization, as the poor and marginalized can gain improved access to government and community resources, their access to which was previously limited. One recurring question is: whether development NGOs themselves are part of civil society? Most NGOs working in development will argue that they are part of civil society, a useful definition of which is: 'that segment of society that interacts with the state, influences the state and yet is distinct from the state' (Chazan 1992: 281). As such, they can play both an empowering and a representative role. However, NGOs generally are not governed or financed on the basis of a membership like a union or a cooperative (Fowler 2000a); and NGO boards tend to be self-appointed, usually from local elites, rather than from a broad membership base (Townsend and Townsend 2004). Thus, it can be easily argued that despite NGOs' own claims to the contrary, in practice they can only play a limited role as civil society representatives (Sabatini 2002; Trivedy and Acharya 1996). Nevertheless there is still ambiguity, as much of the civil society discourse still relates to NGOs as if they are part of civil society (for example, see Finn et al. 2008).

Whether part of civil society or not, NGOs see their role as promoting certain values, and advancing what they see as broader community interests as public benefit organizations, rather than as mutual benefit organizations such as cooperatives or trade unions. For development NGOs, the broader community aspirations they promote include: alleviating poverty; addressing marginalization; achieving social justice; and promoting respect for human rights. The problem with this public benefit role is that NGOs lack a defined accountability path to their constituency, or what Salamon and Anheier (1999: 9) identified as an 'accountability gap'. For example, while NGOs might be advancing the cause of the poor and oppressed, in practice they cannot be held to account by that group on how they advance that cause, nor can the poor and oppressed as a group have much impact on NGOs if they disagree with the strategy and approaches, as the aid recipient has little power in these relationships (Power et al. 2002). This relatively weak accountability relationship is a defining feature of NGOs as public benefit organizations, and has implications for how they work. Couto (1998) has developed a classification for US organizations according to the 'related concepts of participation, representation, community change and empowerment ...' (p. 580). Within the Indian context, his classification can be adapted into the following set of groups:

- *grassroots groups*, which are small community-based, self-help groups which can act for themselves as direct 'socio-political representatives'.
- *community agencies*, which have local decision-making structures, but with little direct representation or full participation of the people served; and
- *voluntary organizations*, larger organizations which generally have no formal feedback mechanisms from the people being served.

The overlapping categories of community organizations and voluntary organizations found in India are typical of the majority of development NGOs in developing countries. They are public benefit organizations, and generally serve as intermediaries between resource providers such as government or other (usually foreign) donors and small community-based organizations or 'grassroots' self-help groups, which while being notionally representative may not have a formal structure or recognition from the state. Aid donors prefer public benefit organizations such as NGOs to undertake broader development work, as they are able to reach a wider and possibly more diverse set of possible aid recipients than membership organizations could, while remaining at arm's length from government:

> the lack of organizational responsiveness and legitimacy [of NGOs] is not only more tolerable than it is in the public sector, but is also a structural prerequisite for coping with the contradictory societal and political demands which, by itself, government cannot resolve.
>
> (Seibel 1990: 114)

NGOs are also seen to be inclusive rather than exclusive in their approach to their aid recipients. They are closer to the communities they are supporting than, say, government agencies, and there are also cost advantages over other delivery mechanisms. These all serve to give NGOs some legitimacy with donors whether these are international or national or state governments (Scurrah 1996). This is on top of the non-economic resources that NGOs have such as status, reputation and information. These can also add to NGO legitimacy, which though can be somewhat shaky in many instances (Ebrahim 2003).

The disadvantage of NGOs undertaking work around empowerment and social change is that they have (at best) limited requirements for formal accountability mechanisms to the local communities and aid recipients, something that should be axiomatic for empowerment, and will be returned to in Chapter 6. Many NGOs in India are aware, however, of the limitations in their accountability structure, and actively promote membership organizations as part of their interventions with a view to the membership organizations taking over the programmes and their ongoing management, but often with limited success. This may be due to NGOs' lack of appreciation of local contexts. For example, while NGO board members see themselves taking on a trusteeship role for the NGO constituency, the perspective they bring is often derived from a values system that has its genesis in a welfare ethic of service provision. This leads to the question of how well NGO board members can reflect the interests of aid recipients (Couto 1998; Howes 1997). This is the central conundrum that NGOs face in being both effective, and able to take on the representational role for their aid recipients, when their motivation and drive comes from values rather than a representative constituency.

NGOs as organizations

NGOs generally emerge from particular social milieus and respond to needs in a particular way; therefore how they see the role of mediating between the citizen and the state is derived from a set of values based on that history and social setting.

The problem then is how NGOs, driven by their own values and altruistic ends, derive their support from a community to undertake this mediation? Couto (1998) argues that it is the representative relationship with the community that determines the effectiveness of the NGO at empowerment or social change. Non-representative NGOs are at best 'technical representatives' (p. 570): while they have a special knowledge of a group, they are not part of it. This distance means NGOs speak on behalf of, rather than as part of the community, which limits their legitimacy (Jordan 2005). I would argue that this gap is due to NGOs as non-representative organizations, deriving a set of values from a certain socio-political milieu that drives their approach to their work. However, it is the very basis of these values (i.e. to work for a larger group in society) and their non-representative nature that raises questions as to the effectiveness of their work (Edwards and Sen 2000; Fowler 1996; Lissner 1977; Power et al. 2002).

The driving force for NGOs as public benefit organizations is that they are essentially motivated by their values, which could be defined broadly into a desire for a 'better world' (Edwards and Sen 2000; Fowler 1996; Lissner 1977). NGOs also regard themselves as 'the heartland of the social economy as they are marked by distinctive value systems ...' (Paton 1993: 6), and they expand 'moral space' (Edwards and Sen 2000: 614). Lissner sums up NGO values thus:

> [they] ... emanate from religious beliefs, historical traditions, prevailing social norms, personal experiences, and similar basic sources of human attitudes, ... cannot be directly translated into concrete action because of their degree of abstraction ... [but provide] bearings when deciding on fundamental directions.
>
> (1977: 74)

Regardless of where these values come from, whether they emerge from religious traditions, paternal leadership, or other sources, it is the values which 'condition the rules of the game' (Fowler 1996: 17). Upholding, or being true to, their values is a primary concern for those NGOs who wish to promote a certain philosophy or worldview – a '*Weltanschauung*' based on these more permanent and deeply held values (Lissner 1977). These *Weltanschauung*-based values are quite different from other types of values that are derived from, for example, supporter interests; third world or recipient interest, which are more temporal; the 'organizational' values that drive the way NGO work is undertaken; or 'terminal' values that indicate an endpoint, such as relief from poverty (Padaki 2000: 424). Table 1 presents a schema of the various sets of values. As ideology or a political goal is the anchor of a political party, values, or a world view, are the anchor for NGOs.

The key problem arising from this discussion is that the values of the NGO may not accord with the values of the aid recipients, in what they aspire to as 'the good life', leading to what can be referred to as a conflict of values (Rose 1980). Many values are normative and not universally held, and so values can be promoted that are inimical to others in society (Fowler 1996). For example, in the Indian context promoting the interests of the marginalized, such as women or *dalits*, can be seen a threat to an existing social order. To some, NGOs may be involved in 'expanding

Table 1 A schema of NGO values

Category of NGO values	Typology
Weltanschauung	Represents a worldview or philosophy, e.g. a religious faith, humanism.
Temporal values	Represents immediate concerns, e.g. humanitarian relief, human rights, self-help, individual autonomy.
Terminal values	Represents an end point to be reached such as an end to poverty; universal education etc., e.g. the Millennium Development Goals.
Organizational values	Represents those of the organization and how it operates, e.g. honesty, integrity, accountability.

Source: Kilby (2006).

moral space' (Edwards and Sen 2000: 614), while to others NGOs may be narrowing a moral space to a particular religious or social ethic, or value system. This leads to a form of moral hazard by which NGOs can articulate their own values and priorities as representing the values and priorities of its constituency, and so consciously or unconsciously gain a benefit in the form either of resources or legitimacy. These can be from either public donors or from the state (Ebrahim 2001; Joshi and Moore 2000).

NGOs and the state

Another school of thought on NGO theory, while not completely at odds with the values-based theory of Lissner, argues that NGOs are by nature in the realm of state influence and control, to the extent that NGOs often behave as proxies for the state (Fowler 2000b; Sen, S. 1999). They argue that there is an informal partnership between the state and NGOs of a mutual interest, and NGOs take on a mediation role (as a service deliverer, and/or policy adviser), between the communities with which they are working and the state (Dutt 2004; Nagar and Raju 2003; Tayler 2005). NGOs gain legitimacy through this work and, at the same time, provide the state with legitimacy. In this way, NGOs start to perform a 'shadow state' function, or become smaller versions of government by providing government services, therefore acting like mini-states without the accountability of a state to its citizens (Sen, S. 1999; Williamson 1991; Zaidi 1999). Any accountability will be mainly towards the state rather than the aid recipients, with the role of values being somewhat diluted. Arguably, this phenomenon of being part of a 'shadow' state affects the larger NGOs in a country like India, with smaller NGOs often able to avoid state scrutiny, but as we shall see in Chapter 3, the smaller NGOs face a different set of influences as both state and donor relations with NGOs undergo rapid change.

It is the political science theories of NGOs (Lissner 1977), which highlight their values base and work for a broader public benefit, that this book will focus on; but it will also note the effects that government and other relations have on NGO behaviour. These different theories of NGOs have a common element and that is that they all point to the multiple accountabilities of NGOs, while at the same time highlighting the fundamental issues for NGOs – which in some ways are their strength – of being driven by values and having a relatively broad constituency of aid recipients. At the same time this can be seen as a weakness, in that the relationship with the aid recipients and local communities they are working with tends to be informal and relatively weak. The next section will explore these issues as they apply to Indian NGOs.

Indian NGOs

Siddhartha Sen (1999) has identified two key features of Indian NGOs involved in development work. The first, is that NGOs play an intermediation role; that is, they work for the poor, rather than being grassroots formations of the poor themselves and; secondly, these NGOs are non-representative organizations. This is in line with the general discussion of NGOs outlined above: while the number of formal members of an NGO is very small (usually from the professional elite), they serve a relatively large number of people in any particular area. They are mainly public benefit organizations rather than representative or mutual benefit organizations, and they are driven by altruistic motives for a broader public benefit.

> In India, [development] NGOs can be defined as organizations that are generally formed by professionals or quasi-professionals from the middle or lower middle classes, either to serve or work with the poor, or to channel financial support to community-based or grassroots organizations of the poor. The NGOs are generally non-membership organizations and have salaried employees.
>
> (Sen, S. 1999: 332)

Indian NGOs have a deep-seated ethical basis for altruism (Baxi 1997; Viswanath 1993). Because of the altruistic motivation, Indian NGOs:

- tend to be relatively conservative and service-oriented;
- are incrementalist (that is, they seek small improvements in people's lives);
- promote non-violence; and
- generally avoid party political processes, and discourage party affiliations.

In terms of a broad values base, Indian NGOs are about the 'existential amelioration of victim groups ... [and] the creation of community solidarity [rather than the] achievement of political emancipation' (Baxi 1997: 56). These values are not static and have evolved from a complex history, which will be discussed in the next section. As Chapters 3 and 4 will demonstrate, Indian NGOs are still evolving in how they respond to global and national circumstances, at the same time maintaining their values.

In the late 1980s, however, Indian NGOs were slowly moving away from directly implementing welfare and income generation programmes, towards more self-help approaches to development, which had been pioneered in the 1970s by NGOs such as MYRADA and SEWA (Self Employed Women's Association) (Viswanath

1993). Whether this change was partly in recognition of the efficacy of the participatory approach, or a response to donor pressure is a moot point. But to some degree this shift did represent an awareness from NGOs of the structural causes of poverty and powerlessness, and that self-help approaches are an important way of addressing the issues of disempowerment (Joseph 1997; Rajasekhar 1998). The self-help group approach very quickly obtained a gender dimension, and self-help approaches were taken up in women's programmes in recognition of the specific disadvantage that women (particularly rural women) faced.

Women's NGOs such as SEWA and Annapurna Mahila Mandal have existed since the 1970s, and the Indian government had established *mahila mandals* (women's groups) in most villages during the 1950s and 1960s. However, it was after the publication in 1987 of the Report of the National Commission on Women 'Sharma Shakti', which focused on the disadvantage that women faced, that the focus on women in self-help programmes took off. As a result of these changes in the 1980s both in the approach of NGOs to women's programmes and the donor support for gender and development, most development NGOs in India since the 1990s have a much stronger focus on self-help approaches, and the specific targeting of women as their primary target group. It is the history and the relationship of NGOs with the Indian state that has shaped Indian development NGOs, and to a large extent influences the approaches they take. This history and experience is unique, not only in South Asia, but arguably in the world. This discussion goes some way to informing how the modern Indian development NGO of the twenty-first century addresses the high levels of poverty in the current development context.

NGOs in India have their origins in ancient times: written in 1,500 BC, the *Rig Veda*, the ancient Aryan Scriptures, promoted the values of *dharma* (personal obligations), *jeev daya* (humanitarian concern and a concern for all living things) and voluntarism and philanthropy (Iyengar 2000; Mishra et al. 2006; Sen, S. 1997). During this earlier period the provision of education, health services, cultural promotion and dealing with natural and other types of emergencies was based on voluntarism rather than being an obligation of the state (Sen, S. 1999), the exception being the Muarya empire of around 300 BC when the state took a strong role (Imandar 1987). This high level of voluntarism was maintained through various Indian empires right up until British colonization in the late eighteenth century. It was out of this history, and the impact of the British colonial administration, that the modern Indian NGO movement was born, but with marked differences after independence in 1947. The pre-independence period, since around 1800, saw the development of a strong NGO sector, which in the latter part of the colonial period took on a strong political dimension, playing an important part in India's independence struggle (Sen, S. 1999; Iyengar 2000). After independence, the development of the NGO sector was characterized by a changing relationship with the state.

NGOs under British colonial rule

In the early nineteenth century, the long standing traditions of voluntarism received a boost from the religious, cultural and social milieu that came from Great Britain as part of its colonial influence. Paradoxically, this was at the expense of the Hindu culture and practices from which the traditions of voluntarism emerged (Imandar 1987). The British influence begun with Christian missionaries from around 1810, and the charity work of the Indian bourgeois class in the 1820s, who came through the British education systems. Both groups had as their primary purpose the provision of welfare; however, some of these groups also had the idea of promoting political empowerment and individual autonomy, an idea which was in part a product of the mission school systems (Sen, S. 1992). A nascent social reform movement emerged with individuals such as Raj Ram Mohan Roy, Brahma Samaj and Arya Samaj protesting against those religious 'evils' that promoted women's subjugation, such as child marriage, dowry and *sati* (ceremonial widow burning). By the 1840s this social reform movement, which started in Bengal, had extended across the sub-continent to western India (Sen, S. 1992; Seth and Sethi 1991). The next change came in the 1860s with the emergence of the first rural self-help groups, and co-operative and credit societies, the precursors of the modern microfinance groups (Sen, S. 1992). Through this early period the colonial government had little direct interaction with these nascent NGOs, but the rapid growth and visibility of NGOs was instrumental in the colonial government introducing the first NGO regulation, in the form of the Public Trust Act and the Societies Registration Act of 1860, providing a legal base for the emerging NGOs (Iyengar 2000).

The next stage in the development of NGOs was the progression from organizations concerned with credit and rural self-help groups, to a movement that also addressed political rights. For example, the Indian National Congress (later to become the Congress Party) was formed in 1885 as an NGO (Markham and Bonjean 1995). The movement for political rights, and the work of Mahatma Gandhi from the turn of the century, resulted in a much stronger political focus for voluntarism, and effectively planted the notion of the liberal tradition of politics more broadly in society. It also provided a historical legitimacy for NGO advocacy (Seth and Sethi 1991), and gave an impetus to the development of the modern NGOs in India, with their strong focus on both social and political change particularly in rural areas (Iyengar 2000). The Gandhian movement not only had a political purpose of getting the British out of India (the Quit India Movement of the 1920s), but it also had a strong village-based social reform agenda based on the notion of *swadeshi* or village self-government and self-sufficiency (Imandar 1987), which shifted the focus of voluntarism from issues-based action to a broader political context (Kudva 2005). The Gandhian movement at the time was funded mainly by urban-based entrepreneurs, and involved large numbers of urban volunteers going out to villages, and joining ashrams to work on social activism and reconstruction programmes: thus becoming the precursors to the modern Indian NGO (Bhattacharya 1987). These groups then built on local grievances to form local organizations that was the basis of the Gandhi's nationalist movement (Spodek 1971). It is an over-statement, however, to suggest nationalism was the main motivation for these local organizations.

In the early days of Gandhi's work in India, the central focus was on the emancipation of peasants at the local level. It was only later that national implications emerged (Brown 1974). Gandhi was able to overcome the diverging social groups that made up Indian society at the time to unite them with a common focus, and this was largely due to the network of local organizations he was able to set up (Kumar 1969). The key shortcoming of Gandhi's model was that it was reluctant to network outside its own base to non-Gandhian groups; and it was relatively weak institutionally, with alliances forged among diverse social groups quickly disintegrating when obstacles emerged. The Gandhians seemed to lack the processes necessary for renewal and providing ongoing institutional support, and ultimately the ashram model as a development agent was not sustainable. In the 1960s and 1970s it became vulnerable to state intervention and stagnation (Sen, S. 1992).

Another source of activism in the early part of the nineteenth century was from the many Marxist groups who built trade unions or *kisan-sabhas* at grassroots level. Despite strong political differences between the Gandhian and the Marxist groups, the colonial state was not able to isolate or divide them, even though they seldom cooperated. It was the strong support by the Gandhian and the Marxist NGOs for the independence movement that became the basis of close collaboration between the postcolonial Indian government and the NGOs following independence, and throughout the 1950s. There was, however, a third group of NGOs that did not challenge the legitimacy of the colonial state, preferring social rather than political reform and seeing themselves (in the 1920s) primarily as welfare- or service-based. They received grants-in-aid from the colonial state on condition they did not support the Quit India Movement, and so became the first recipients of government funding for NGOs in India (Dhanagare 1990).

NGOs after independence

In the post-independence period, we can say the history of NGO and state relations falls into three broad eras: an era of co-operation from independence until the late 1950s; an era of antagonism from the early 1960s until the late 1970s; and finally, an era of relatively strong state control of NGOs from the mid-1980s to the present day (Jain 1997). In reality, the elements of co-operation, antagonism and state control have been present to varying degrees throughout the history of development NGOs in India, but in the fifty years since independence these broad trends can be discerned.

1947–1960 – 'the honeymoon'

NGO work in the immediate post-independence period was characterized by close co-operation with the state, coming from the euphoria brought about by independence, and the role NGOs, particularly the Gandhian organizations, had in achieving it. It was also related to the Gandhian development paradigm built around village development, which offered a way of reaching the marginalized rural poor who were in a desperate situation at the time, having suffered decades of neglect by the colonial state (Jain 1997). What the NGOs brought to the table was a unique expertise in community mobilization and service delivery at village level, which the state did not have, and so the Indian government began funding NGOs from the first five-year plan. In return, the NGOs became a form of 'shadow state' and offered little opposition to state development policies (Sen, S. 1992: 336). They provided services to substitute or supplement government efforts, and tended not to criticize government.

The main actors in this period were the Gandhian organizations, which played an important role in the independence struggle and, as a consequence, were close to government. They were involved mainly in training government officials and in promoting village-based industry (Sen, S. 1992), and were involved in the establishment of the two government authorities, the Khadi and Village Industries Commission (KVIC) and the Central Social Welfare Board (CSWB). They both became mechanisms for funding NGOs to develop village associations (Chowdry 1987; Nanavatty 1987); but neither body provided an avenue for sustaining NGOs. Over 35 years the CSWB set up 10,000 organizations, but only provided funding for programmes not infrastructure, leading to a permanent dependency on CSWB programmes for survival (Nanavatty 1987), and as a consequence less than 10 per cent have survived into the twenty-first century (Mishra et al. 2006).

During the 1950s, voluntary financial support from the business sector, which sustained NGOs prior to independence, fell away as it was replaced by an increase in state funding (Iyengar 2000). This led to a rapid growth in the number of NGOs through the 1950s and into the 1960s. The range of NGOs also broadened to include welfare groups; NGOs formed by international counterparts; non-party political action groups; and those helped by local government and other local NGOs. The rapid growth in the number and influence of NGOs in the broader community sowed the seeds for disillusionment, by both government and the NGOs, in how each saw the other's role and effectiveness in their interactions with society. NGOs began to see the state funding of NGO programmes as a process of the government fostering co-option and dependency, leading to resentment and hostility from many NGOs to the strong statist agenda being set. The state on its part saw the NGOs as being both inefficient and to a certain extent non-compliant or even unco-operative, in implementing the government's agenda (Sen, S. 1999) – it was perceived by the Indian government that NGOs promised much, but delivered considerably less. This disillusionment by the NGOs and the Indian state led to increasing resistance to broader state policies, especially those promoting rapid industrialization and urbanization, and an increase in antagonism between the state and NGOs.

1960s and 1970s – the estrangement

In the 1960s, a young dissatisfied middle class began to set up alternative NGO formations, which were more radical and movement-based. These young people were at odds with the model of development being adopted by the state, one which was seen to be increasing the gap between rich and poor. Many international NGO donors in the West, in response to the calls for action as part of the United Nations' First Development Decade, at the same time encouraged their Indian counterparts to adopt alternative development models based on village-level formations, also as a counter to the centralized socialist state model that India was partially adopting. However, the most radical shift was the growth of the *sarvodaya* movement led by Jayaprakash Narayan and Vinova Bhave, calling for a radical revolution, involving inter alia the voluntary redistribution of land based on principles of Gandhian socialism (Mishra et al. 2006; Sen, S. 1992).

By the early 1970s some NGOs actively entered the political arena by rallying around Jayaprakash and the *sarvodaya* movement and campaigning against the government of the then Prime Minister, Indira Gandhi. This political campaign peaked during the government 'emergency' of 1975–77, when a state of emergency was declared, elections cancelled and the Parliament by-passed, with the Prime Minister ruling by decree. This led to an intense struggle between the NGOs and the government, with many NGO leaders imprisoned. The defeat of the Indira Gandhi government in 1977 provided a reprieve for the NGOs as the new Janata Party government, which included many Gandhians, provided an environment for the growth of activist NGOs (Baxi 1997; Mishra et al. 2006) and an increase in government support for NGOs (Sen, S. 1992). The Janata government, however, was short-lived, being defeated in 1980 by a vengeful Congress Party, which brought in the era of state control of NGOs.

1980s to 2000s – the new dispensation: more state control

The 30 years since the 1980 elections have seen a re-evaluation of the relationship between the state and NGOs. The romanticism of the 1950s and 1960s is long gone, and the perceived threat to the state that NGOs posed in the 1970s casts a long shadow, and to some extent is still present. As a result of this history, the process of the tightening of NGO regulations in India has been slow, ongoing and deliberate. The first step in the process started earlier when the first Indira Ghandi government passed the Foreign Contributions Regulation Act (FCRA) in 1976, after three years of consultation and parliamentary committee work. The purpose of the FCRA was to ensure that foreign funds were used for purposes consistent with the sovereignty of the Indian republic, and in line with Indian law. Its genesis was in 1969 when there was a suspicion that foreign organizations, including the CIA, were providing funding for trade unions, student bodies and others for what could be seen as subversive activities (Ministry of Home Affairs 2008). The Act at the time, however, was aimed at the more political-based organizations rather than NGOs per se (Jalali 2008).

The second Indira Gandhi government of 1980 gave formal recognition to NGOs as development actors, but still saw them as a threat (Jain 1997). As a consequence, the government put in train a number of laws and procedures to further regulate, and arguably intimidate NGOs; one effect was that the reformist activism of the 1960s was branded as 'revolutionary politics' and proscribed (Baxi 1997: 60). The first major legal change to the regulation of NGOs by the central government was the enactment of the Finance Act of 1983 to remove tax deductibility for corporate donations, and income from any business activities undertaken by NGOs. A little later, in 1985, there was also a further tightening of the provisions of the FCRA to bring NGOs more directly into its purview, inter alia: to bring funds received by third parties to give to NGOs into the Act; broaden the definition of political parties (to include NGOs); ensure that foreign funds were received only after registration and only through designated bank accounts; and allow Central government to inspect and audit books of accounts of organizations (Ministry of Home Affairs 2008). This latter provision meant annual inspections and interviews by the Central Bureau of Intelligence – a federal police function (Chowdry 1987; Puroshothaman 1998). Under the Act the government was given the ability to withdraw FCRA approval for somewhat vague and ill-defined reasons including:

> If the acceptance of foreign contribution by the association is likely to be prejudicial to (a) the sovereignty and integrity of India; (b) free and fair elections to any Legislature or House of Parliament; (c) public interest; (d) friendly relations with a foreign state; or (e) harmony between any religious, social, linguistic, regional groups, caste or community.
>
> (Ministry of Home Affairs 2007: 6)

At the same time, and somewhat paradoxically, the state continued to recognize the important role that NGOs could play in service delivery at village level, in part to ameliorate the perceived failings of the central government. The state benefited because it quarantined the NGOs' work to the village level to deal with local level issues around services, which the centralized state was unable to administer effectively, while it limited NGOs' voice on national issues (Kothari 1987). The government of India's funding to NGOs for this work was strictly for service programmes. For example, in 1980, with the Sixth Five Year Plan (1980–1985), the government identified new areas in which NGOs as new actors could participate in development: the optimal utilization and development of renewable sources of energy, including forestry, through the formation of renewable energy associations at the block level; family welfare, health and nutrition, education and relevant community programmes in the field; health for all programmes; water management and soil conservation; social welfare programmes for 'weaker sections'; implementation of minimum needs programmes; disaster preparedness and management (i.e. for floods, cyclones, etc.); promotion of ecology and tribal development: and environmental protection and education (Mohanty and Singh 2001). However, little funding was available for capacity building, institutional development, or rights and empowerment type activities, as they were seen to be political in nature. By the late 1990s there were not only considerable delays in obtaining FCRA approval, but a number of NGOs had their FCRA permission threatened on the grounds of the 'political' nature of their work:

> ... depending on the character of the issue, states may facilitate and encourage foreign ties of some domestic actors ... while prohibiting the transnational links of other actors.
>
> (Jalali 2008: 166)

The other major action of the government towards NGOs in the early 1980s was a campaign of official harassment. This was mainly in the form of the Kudal Commission, a Presidential Commission to investigate the activities of the Gandhi Peace Foundation, an umbrella organization for 945 Gandhian NGOs. The constant scrutiny, public hearings, hostile media campaigns and accusations throughout the period of the Commission resulted in what Chaturvedi (1987: 542) describes as the NGOs becoming 'distracted and confused' and much less inclined to be involved in national-level advocacy work. At the end of five years of investigation the Kudal Commission found nothing untoward in the work of the Gandhi Peace Foundation and other NGOs, and no charges were laid; but it only came to an end when a new generation of younger NGO leaders pressured the government to have it closed down (Sen, S. 1999).

While the Kudal Commission was the 'stick' against NGOs, the 'carrot' was substantially increased funding to NGOs for specific programmes. The catch was that NGOs were defined very narrowly as ' politically neutral development organizations which would help the government and its rural development programmes' (from the GOI Seventh Five Year Plan [1985–90], quoted in (Sen 1999: 342). This new dispensation provided little space for social movements or advocacy; but on the other hand government funding to NGOs was increased to $US172m. This increase in government largesse to NGOs, combined with the controls on foreign funding, effectively meant the government had got its way and had 'co-opted, controlled, and curbed voluntary organizations' (Chaturvedi 1987: 543). They had used coercion to achieve compliance through the threat of alienation; while at the same time using remuneration to achieve a more 'calculative compliance' (Bhattacharya 1987: 383). This process throughout the 1980s resembled a state version of the 'good cop – bad cop' routine.

The curbing of NGOs at the national level resulted in a relatively disunited and disempowered NGO movement by the end of the 1980s. NGO advocacy work was directed at the state and local government level, rather than the national government (Jenkins 1998). This was of immense advantage to the economic reformers in the Central government, as it diverted the targets of dissent to state and local level political processes, unlike the 1960s and 1970s when the Centre was the target for NGO advocacy. As well as the controls and the pressure by the government, this more conservative shift was helped by the disintegration of the more radical groups and the left agenda, and the entry of young more technocratic professionals into the NGO sector (Sen, S. 1992). The Gandhian and radical politics-based values of the 1950s and 1960s were fading quickly and the new emergent NGOs had their philosophical basis more in the field of social work, where social change and social mobilization were becoming more widely accepted as part of social work teaching (Siddiqui 1997).

State scrutiny and increased funding saw two groups of NGOs emerge: those that were more action-oriented; and those that were welfare-oriented (Kaushik 1997). The latter group saw themselves as intermediaries between donors and the poor as 'aid managers', or as Sen sardonically calls them, the 'technical branch of the poor' (Sen, S. 1992: 184): they provided services such as health and education to the poor and avoided political processes of any sort. The action-oriented groups were involved in empowerment and networking at a local level (Joshi 2003; Murthy and Rao 1997). While there was a political dimension in dealing with issues around empowerment, people's rights and related issues, there was also a clear move away from national-level activism to a more local and community-based level of political activity. At a practical level these NGOs trod the fine line of not antagonizing local-level political figures enough that they would take their concerns to the Ministry of Home Affairs (national government) and have the NGOs' accreditation threatened.

The 1990s were seen to herald a new era of state-NGO cooperation, in which the centrepiece was a two-day Planning Commission meeting with 100 NGOs held in 1994 and chaired by Prime Minister P.V. Narasimha Rao. The agreement from the meeting was an Action Plan to strengthen relations between government and NGOs, and set up consultative machinery; but there was no agreement to simplify the contentious FCRA procedures (Joshi 2003). The Plan saw NGOs having two main roles – the delivery of services (rather than supplementing existing services) and the empowerment of marginalized groups. This new rapprochement was put under some strain when the NGOs had their credibility dented by a number of financial scandals. In 1996 the Council for Advancement of People's Action and Rural Technology (CAPART) audited 2,000 of the 7,500 NGOs which it supported and found fraud to the value of Rs50 crore ($US10m), 300 non-existent or phantom NGOs (Murthy and Rao 1997: 66) and 26 other NGOs engaging in criminal conspiracy to defraud (Bava 1997: 271). These scandals led to further distrust of NGOs, not only on political grounds but also on ethical grounds, bringing into question their role as advocates. The chequered history of NGOs in the 1980s and 1990s sets the scene for the contemporary NGO movement, and how it responds in its work to multiple pressures of accountability while at the same time having a role in the empowerment of the poor and marginalized.

NGOs in India today

The vibrant history of Indian NGOs in the 60 years since independence has resulted in a more broad-based sector, but one that still has to contend with problems of autonomy and independence. While the Indian state does not exert absolute control over the NGO sector, it is able to keep it in check and away from the national-level political processes, and in effect set limits on NGOs' role as empowerment agents. There are two major trends in Indian civil society that have had an effect on development NGOs in the 2000s: first, the activist groups of the 1960s and 1970s have abandoned the NGO as an institutional form, preferring informal networks that are completely separate from the state regulatory frameworks and scrutiny, seeing the state as inherently oppressive and not to be trusted (Chandhoke and Ghosh 1995; Murthy and Rao 1997; Seth and Sethi 1991). However, the price they pay is that they remain small-scale due to the very restricted access to resources (Murthy and Rao 1997). The second trend is the emergence of funda-mentalist movements such as the *Hindutva* (Hindu nationalist movement) that are fundamentally undemocratic, opposing rational discourse based on freedom and equality (Chandhoke 1995). Neither of these two changes help in having NGOs engage in civil society processes: the total disengagement from the state weakens the process for holding the state accountable, and the move to an intolerance of diversity of discourse narrows the parameters in which the state can be engaged. NGOs are affected either way, as they feel any engagement with the state on policy issues will draw hostile attention from both social action groups on the one hand and the fundamentalists on the other. Now that social activists and fundamentalists both occupy the political stage, NGOs feel their role is now in helping marginalized groups advance their own interests and assert their rights themselves.

There is also a growing vulnerability of NGOs – particularly larger ones that are dependent on foreign funding – to state scrutiny and the state's capacity to cut off NGO resources. An example of this is that the dependent relationship between NGOs and the state has limited the level of networking among NGOs, due to competition among them for resources from the state and foreign sources, and a fall in foreign funding sources in the 2000s. The less supportive environment for NGOs has brought some of their less favourable characteristics more to the fore: inflexibility, a feudal management style – being dominated by powerful individuals with little devolution of power, and recruitment very much caste- or personally based (Reddy 1987). Whether these characteristics are unique to NGOs or are more or less an inherent style of institutional management in India is another matter. The other side of this coin is that the decline in foreign funding relative to local funding, together with deregulated international financial flows, may make it more difficult for NGOs to gain greater autonomy from the state, especially if they are social change agents with broader empowerment objectives. The regulatory pressures on NGOs through amendments to the FCRA have been tightening; for example, in 2001 the Law Commission of India was commissioned by government to prepare a series of amendments to the FCRA): these were finally tabled in the Lok Sabha (Parliament) in 2006. Earlier amendments had already resulted in substantial tightening; for example, all applicants for FCRA approval must obtain an affidavit from the district administrator explaining the nature of their past and current activities. The 2006 draft amendment proposed a further a tightening of FCRA including: the renewing of FCRA registration every five years; stronger restrictions on engaging in religious conversion activities but with vague definitions of the key terms 'inducement', or 'indirectly inducing a conversion'; a forward looking clause in which the certifying officer had to make a judgment on the likelihood of non-compliance and whether a 'meaningful' project had been prepared; a cap on administration expenses but with no supporting definitions; and finally the provision for the state to dispose of assets purchased through foreign donations, something that could put schools and hospitals at risk if they had changed hands in any way (Jalali 2008; Parker 2007). On financial matters, an amendment in 2008 sought to remove the overall tax exemption, if there are any business activities at all, and these could include any cost recovery activities such as fees for running trainings and the like (AccountAble 2008). These changes mirror a broader questioning globally of the purpose (and legitimacy) of NGOs, and a tightening of NGOs' administration, marking the relationship of the state to NGOs in the opening years of the twenty-first century as one of mutual suspicion and a strongly instrumentalist view of what NGOs are or should do (Jalali 2008; Kilby 2004).

NGOs and community development

These features of the Indian NGO sector in the early 2000s present both challenges and opportunities for more effective community development programming and empowerment, the key role that NGOs have taken for themselves. The policy for greater decentralization to local-level government, under the Panchayat Raj Act of 1992, has resulted in growing numbers of local-level NGOs. The population for each village Panchayat is now 5,000 people (down from 10,000) while at the same time village government is now responsible for a larger budget and a broader range of activities including water supply, village roads, community amenities and broader development activities. This has provided NGOs with the opportunity to be not only service providers, but also monitors and mediators of the process; and in themselves facilitators of local-level activism and local-level power politics through their empowerment programmes. Because local NGOs are less visible than their national-level counterparts, they are able to take on some of the more sensitive advocacy roles, albeit at a local level. What has emerged is a large area of overlap, in which NGOs are able to meet social change objectives such as empowerment *through* service delivery (Sen, S. 1999). This, however, leads to a relatively simplistic interpretation of the term 'empowerment', avoiding the analysis of power relations inherent in the term. To be fair, a blended approach is also driven by the pragmatics of working with poor people who require tangible benefits, without which any interaction is seen as a waste of their time.

Against this suspicion by the state of NGO empowerment programmes, there is an increasing official donor awareness that effective poverty alleviation requires, at the bare minimum, the participation of beneficiaries in development activities rather than their being passive recipients. While the Indian state has effectively kept NGOs out of many broader political debates, at the local level there are greater opportunities for NGOs to use modes of intervention that enable both service delivery and empowerment, largely free of state scrutiny. The hostile state can also have the effect of forcing NGOs to be less spokespeople for the poor, and more mediators or facilitators to enable the poor and marginalized to speak for themselves. This is something that if left alone NGOs are generally not good at, as they can exacerbate rather than mitigate the exclusion of the poor from the political processes by fostering a level of dependency on them to carry out this role; raising the obvious question of the extent to which these small local groups can be empowered if they cannot pose a threat to the larger NGO (Kaushik 1997). This is an important outcome for the empowerment of the poor, as NGOs can deflect state scrutiny away from themselves to the small, informal and locally based representative organizations they may be working with (Rajasekhar 1998). The move to more local-level NGOs can still lead to co-option when they engage with the state, raising the question of whether their role is to go further and mediate conflicts between those with vested interests and the poor, and so be forced to take positions. Localization of NGOs also weakens opportunities for networking when they live in a competitive environment for resources, making the overall NGO reach small and fragmented (Murthy and Rao 1997). Likewise, the assumed comparative advantage of smaller NGOs being closer to the poor is compromised by more scrutiny and funding from more local-level political processes. The notions of equality, mutuality and trust may be difficult to maintain, and contribute to an alienation of the NGOs from their constituency, thus limiting their capacity for empowerment.

The discussion of the pressures that Indian NGOs have been under over the past 20 years highlights the point that for many the values base of social change for many NGOs has been threatened by the imperative for survival and income. Arguably, the move to smaller local-level NGOs provides an opportunity for the flexibility for effective empowerment programme and stronger accountability links to their constituents. However, the pressures from local-level governments and donors place limits on this process for a fragmented set of NGO players.

Effectiveness of Indian NGOs

The key issue for NGO effectiveness that this volume examines is empowerment – the expansion of choice and autonomous action for women, the major constituent group for NGO work in India. A key issue is the institutional capacity of the very poor to manage certain (mainly administrative) processes, and thus a level of dependency is developed in which the very poor will tend to use the NGO for institutional support and thus make the NGO seem indispensable in the community, possibly leading to a disempowering relationship (Murthy and Rao 1997). The other issue is one of targeting, and whether NGOs are reaching the very poor. In one study only one-third of NGO programmes were found to reach the very poor and most marginalized groups, and the level of targeting of landless, *dalits*, poor women and poor Muslims was less than their proportion in the total population. In other words, the programmes were inequitable and discriminating (unintentionally) against the very poor they were meant to help. Murthy and Rao (1997) went on, however, to note that at least NGOs are better at targeting the poor than the government: NGOs reached 80–100 per cent of the poor, and government programmes reached 60–80 per cent.

Gender and NGO effectiveness

One of the paradoxes facing 'empowerment' NGOs in India is that the one area where government scrutiny and threat is less, but where NGOs are still slow to react, is gender. In particular, there is a poor response by NGOs to the difficulties faced by women in rural India in disempowerment, and the concomitant lack of access to both resources and decision-making. While government programmes have been targeting disadvantaged women since the 1970s, which produced The Status of Women Committee Report, a benchmark document in the 1970s, and again in 1992 The Respective Plan for Women led to a Statutory Commission for women, at that time there were very few NGO targeting programmes for women in general, or rural women in particular. The exceptions were a few notable women's NGOs such as the Self-employed Women's Association (SEWA) and Annapurna Mahila Mandal (both urban based). It was not until the late 1980s that rural NGOs with a majority constituency of women emerged (Viswanath 1993).

In the 1980s there are two general types of NGOs that work with women: institutions in the form of service/welfare oriented hostels for working women; and those NGO programmes that were 'struggle-oriented' – helping women assert their rights (Viswanath 1993), but in the early 2000s this shifted, with most NGOs in India targeting women at a practical level such as microfinance or income generation. Fewer NGOs directly address gender-based violence, alcoholism, access to work and other strategic gender needs. While there are movements around these issues, these are led by powerful individuals or political groups, rather than NGOs per se; and even fewer NGOs address opportunities for broader political participation or women. When the factors of both a poor poverty focus and inadequate gender approaches are taken together, it is the most marginalized women, *dalits* and tribals who are worse off (Murthy and Rao 1997). While it may go without saying that empowerment programmes have to deal with disempowerment and power relations, both at a personal level and more broadly in terms of the level of social marginalization that women face, it is difficult to find a concerted movement among NGOs to do so. If empowerment is being able to have extended choices, and being able to act on those choices in a number of domains, then how the NGOs work with the most disadvantaged groups, and support them to deal with their own issues, is a key element of any intervention – which brings us to the vexed question of NGO accountability.

Accountability and Indian NGOs

The issue of the accountability of Indian NGOs is usually discussed in terms of their accountability to donors or the state, and it is this compliance of NGOs to state and donor pressure that has left them out of touch with their aid recipients:

> ... when the activist [NGO] is not regarded as worthy of state repression, but when the people alongside her are repressed and brutally so the problems of accountability [to the aid recipient] assume terrifying dimensions.
>
> (Baxi 1997: 63)

The question then is what works for NGOs in terms of their accountability to their aid recipients. Devolved management structures can give greater opportunity for participation of membership and responsiveness of the organizations, that is: if the NGO listens to its members; whether it shares power; and whether it provides timely support. Smith-Sreen (1995) found that high levels of accountability were correlated with higher economic benefits and medium social benefits, while low levels of member accountability were associated with both low economic and social benefits. Five factors seem to have an effect on the accountability of NGOs to their members:

- socio-cultural environment, that is the history and goals of the organization concerned;
- NGO's resources in terms of staff, membership, and funds;
- organizational structure of the NGO including the board, its activities and external influences such as donors;
- organizational strategy, that is the norms and values, and leadership style, and
- organizational processes such as the group formation and co-ordinating mechanisms.

(Smith-Sreen 1995: 92)

In the case of PREM in Orissa, Edwards (1999b) found that when the NGO reduced its role as intermediary and handed over control to smaller representative organizations, this was an empowering process. On the other hand the 'oligarchic tendencies' (Sheth 1996: 133) of NGOs to take on a representative role themselves can weaken the collective empowerment of communities (Pantoja 1999). Without constant pressure from below NGOs can assume a paternalistic role and a shift in priorities (Rajasekhar 2000). The complex relationship NGOs have with their constituencies is important as the notion of accountability of NGOs to constituencies (a 'downward accountability'), and how NGOs foster autonomy of the constituencies in a range of areas, is central to the idea of empowerment.

Conclusion

This chapter has drawn together a number of strands to provide a context for the detailed look at the local NGOs in India that this book focuses on. The theory of NGOs as values-based organizations with a number of competing accountability pressures is a real one, but this is tempered in the Indian context by the long history of NGOs in India which, together with the on-going tension between the state and NGOs over the past 50 years, has created a complex and moving mosaic of NGOs formations and NGO state relations, the main one being a strong local focus. The tensions between the state and the NGOs provide a number of important challenges for NGOs if they are to have an impact on the levels of poverty that exist in India and particularly among marginalized women in rural India. The Indian experience, particularly the dilemmas outlined above, is important for the study as it highlights the organizational issues that NGOs face if they are to be effective. The key questions that have emerged of Indian NGOs are those of identity and focus. Should the focus of NGO work should be around service delivery, which is the model favoured by the state as it hands over services to NGOs in response to economic pressures? Or should NGOs be involved in empowerment programmes that focus on the poor and marginalized claiming their rights from the state? If the focus is on empowerment then NGOs face issues around scale and internal management structures, particularly their accountability mechanisms. These questions, then, are on the role of accountability in empowerment; and secondly, the effect of the range of accountability relationships that NGOs have, and how these relationships affect their accountability to the aid recipients.

2 The work of NGOs in India – SHGs and women's empowerment

Introduction

Chapter 1 outlined the broad history of Indian NGOs over the past 100 years and the factors that have brought them to where they are in India's national development. The particular focus has been on the past 50 years and the role NGOs have assumed in modern Indian society, especially the relationships they have developed with government, which served both as regulator and supporter. The focus will now shift to India in the early 2000s and how NGOs are situated in the broader development scene in India, and in particular, look at their modes of operation and the approaches they have adopted in order to be effective. The main development approach for NGOs working with local communities that has emerged over the past 30 years is through self-help groups (SHG). This approach originated in Karnataka in the mid-1970s, has since been widely adopted by NGOs across the country and is now strongly supported by government through its national five-year development plans (Fernandez 2001). The SHG movement distinguishes itself from other models of social organization for development programmes in that it, in theory at least, is less about the delivery of services and more about the empowerment of group members to be able to make and act on expanded choices, and so advance their interests.

Given that empowerment is seen as a central feature of NGO activity, even if only aspirationally, it is important then to examine what empowerment is about. As a starting point I will argue that empowerment can only be analysed through the lens of disempowerment, which directly links to approaches to poverty and marginalization. These contested terms are often treated in development discourse as a 'given', but they need to be deconstructed to understand exactly what they mean, and then examine how NGOs and SHGs deal with them. This chapter will set the context by looking at the drivers of poverty in India, the nature of empowerment, and finally the self-help group approach that NGOs use for empowerment and poverty alleviation.

Poverty in India

India is a country of just over 1 billion people, of whom 26 per cent live in poverty, when the national measure of a minimum calorie intake of 2,400 calories per person in rural areas and 2,100 calories in urban areas is applied (CIA 2008; Deaton and

Dreze 2002). While aggregate poverty figures based on household food consumption hide many dimensions of poverty, they do provide a broad sketch of where poverty in India is, particularly compared to the past (Loughhead et al. 2001). The important institutional features of the poverty data for India are: very large regional differences in the incidence of poverty, mainly between the north and the south of India, with higher concentrations of poverty in the north (Murthi et al. 1996); and worsening income inequality, rising by 10 per cent in the 1990s (Deaton and Dreze 2002). Finally, if the definition of poverty is broadened to include other indicators such as education and health, as the UNDP Human Development Index does, then the figure for India would be somewhat higher, with 32 per cent of households living in poverty in 2003 (UNDP 2008).

But these figures tell us little about vulnerability, of who is falling in and out of poverty (and why) at any point in time: for example, in a study of 36 villages in Andhra Pradesh, the level of poverty fell two per cent over a 25-year period, but it was not the steady (if not glacial) fall that a figure of a two per cent fall suggests. In that 25-year period, 14 per cent of households came out of poverty and 12 per cent of households fell into poverty – in all 26 per cent of households experienced changes in their poverty levels (Krishna 2006). What the figures mask is the high level of vulnerability these communities were facing, which is harder to measure:

> The identification of vulnerable households [is] more difficult than that of poor households since a household's vulnerability depends in large measure on the severity of the shock to which it is exposed.
>
> (Gaiha and Imai 2004: 261)

The sources of vulnerability include shock-induced poverty, which is a result of household-level problems like income loss and asset destruction, and recovery problems, often called *idiosyncratic vulnerability*: these problems can come from disease epidemics, cost of health care, death and funeral expenses, theft and violence, and the shocks from globalization such as super-inflation, job loss, not getting paid, etc. There is also the vulnerability that whole communities face, often called *covariate vulnerability*, which includes floods, drought and the like (Maxwell et al. 2008). Entitlement vulnerability has to do with a lack of access to other and more rewarding options especially during a crisis; for example, the lack of strong labour laws and the lack of recognition of workers' rights in the context of increased short-term migration. (Wonink et al. 2005). This is also related to endogenous factors such as caste, education levels and gender, as they determine 'who has assets, who can access public facilities, who has political connections and who has supportive social networks' (Bosher et al. 2007: 615).

Despite the rapid and impressive growth in India over the past 20 years, the issue of chronic poverty is still a serious problem, historically in rural areas where growth has not been able to match the rates in urban areas, due to a stagnation of investment in the rural sector by successive governments (Jha 2002). In the early 2000s, however, chronic poverty was increasing in urban areas due to poor job security and higher costs of living (Loughhead et al. 2001). Despite the relatively weak rural sector in India there is still, however, a relatively low and slow level of urbanization, with only 28 per cent of the population urbanized and 60 per cent still living in villages of fewer than 5,000 people. The rate of urbanization was 12 per cent in India in 1900 and has only doubled over the century (Datta 2006). This slow rate of urbanization may be due both to the strong and largely conservative social structures which underpin Indian villages, and the greater vulnerability and lack of support structures in urban areas. Whatever the causes for these slow social changes, for the poor there are fundamental structural issues that have to be overcome, if there are to be significant improvements in overall poverty levels. Some of these structural issues have a lot to do with how village societies are organized, to which addressing the marginalized role of women in these societies is key.

> In large areas of India women live with many burdens and fears. They carry the burden of neglect and discrimination, household work, looking after siblings and of work outside the home. As girls they live with the fear of not getting adequate attention, care, nourishment, medical attention and education. With adolescence comes the fear of being sold, sometimes sold in the name of marriage, sometimes sold into child labour and prostitution. After marriage a girl's status descends to an even lower level and her subservience becomes institutionalized. There is also fear of loneliness, maladjustments, not being allowed a personhood, mental torture and harassment, and occasionally even death – murder by her own people.
>
> (Janardhan 1995: 39)

The improvements in the level of poverty in India over the past two decades mask some of the ingrained institutional barriers that prevent marginalized groups such as *dalits*, scheduled tribes and women from converting any increased income they should be receiving, either from the state as welfare, or from their families, to access basic needs (Mehta and Shah 2003). If we look at gender disparities, a focus of this book, the poverty levels for female-headed households in India are a full 20 per cent higher than the national average, and the story is similar for inequality levels (Meenakshi and Ray 2003; Sen and Mukherjee 2006). One way of measuring the extent of gender disadvantage is the sex ratio of females to males, which points to a systemic societal bias towards men and boys in all aspects of the life cycle. Because of women's greater longevity the norm should be a little more than 1000 women per 1000 men, but for India in 2001 it was a low 933 females per 1000 males (the lowest for all major countries). The lower ratio for India is due to higher mortality rates for females than males in all age cohorts as a result of the discrimination and violence Indian women experience throughout their lifecycle; and this ratio is getting worse over time (the figure for in India in 1901 was 972 females per 1000 males (Census of India 2001: 3).

Women live with many of Janardhan's burdens and fears, and these play out to create what Amartya Sen call the 'missing women'; the women who otherwise should be alive. Selective abortion (increasingly common in India as the price of an amniocentesis falls) is but one reason for the 'missing women'. The social disadvantage suffered by women is by far a greater contributing factor. Some of the statistics that point to the extent of disadvantage are: the earned income for women is 34 per cent of that for men; the adult literacy ratio for women is 70 per cent of that for men; primary school enrolment for girls is 85 per cent of that for boys; high school enrolment ratio is 80 per cent; tertiary enrolment ratio is 70 per cent, and so on (UNDP 2008). These statistics point to an 'unequal allocation of food, lower wage rates and a lack of inheritance rights' (Mehta and Shah 2003: 503). In short, it means poorer life outcomes for women relative to men. These gender biases go well beyond the household, as women have a lower level of both legal and normative entitlements to ownership and exchange of both land and produce. This leads to exchange failures for women in terms of the prices they receive for their produce and their labour; their social relations within the household and the village; and finally, in terms of the claims that women can make on the state for welfare and other benefits. As if this were not enough, there are also large differences in endowments between men and women to access assets and control their labour; as well as differences in their status, access to training to upgrade their skills, and access to inputs for agriculture and other income generation activities. While there have been improvements over the past decade, there is still some way to go to overcome the institutionalized disadvantage for Indian women.

These persisting social barriers have been exacerbated since the 1990s by a trend to greater fragmentation in Indian society exemplified by the rise of the Hindu nationalist movement, *hindutva*, which has produced more caste, ethnic and religious conflict, and led to an increased disenfranchisement of minorities such as Muslims, tribals and *dalits*; and with it a reasserting of more traditional gender roles (Das 2008). This more conservative shift tends to weaken the capacity for women to be heard at the political level, leading to greater levels of intolerance and increased denial of rights at the local level. On the other hand, religious fundamentalism is attractive to those women who regard modernization as a chaotic and unsettling process, as fundamentalism provides some compensation and a refuge. The *hindutva* has afforded new 'safer' roles and status for women, such as performing Hindu rituals and meeting with other women on religious issues. This has the effect of elevating their self-worth at an individual level, and at the same time changing the woman's role in public spaces from a social or even political one, to a religious one. In this context, work outside the home is seen as a poverty-driven coping strategy or a desperation measure, rather than as a springboard to escape poverty (Parker et al. 2003). This new dispensation ensures that the traditional roles, duties and responsibilities of women remain firmly in place, and it sets out boundaries as to how far 'empowerment' and other social progress for women can go. Dress codes, for example, become important, along with marriage alliances and feminine 'modesty', which to some might be seen as code for submissiveness, and to 'uphold the patriarchal family and to be the ideal wife/daughter/sister/mother ...' (Srinivasan 2007: 126).

Poverty and the political reforms of the 1990s

One of the sources of the modernizing change that has reduced poverty levels in India, these reforms were effectively forced on the government by the mounting debt of the 1980s when the foreign debt for India rose from 17.7 per cent of GNP to an unsustainable 24.8 per cent in 1990. Not only was there a dramatic increase in the levels of debt but the type of debt also changed from long-term concessional government debt, to short-term and higher risk private debt. This level of debt, together with government current expenditure at unacceptable levels, was leading the country to an economic crash, and the associated loss of confidence in the economy (Panagariya 2004). As a result emergency provisions were put in place and a number of government controls were removed: changes included relaxing the terms of investment, easing the regulations on the ownership of assets and land, partially floating the exchange rates, and privatizing some public assets and functions. The immediate effect was a sharp rise in rural poverty from 35 per cent to 44 per cent in the first two years following the reforms, with the landless, casual labour and women-headed households being hardest hit (Jha 2002). The proportion of women in paid employment fell from 28 per cent to 23 per cent (Murthy and Rao 1997). The benefit, however, was that over the next decade goods and services trade nearly doubled from 17 to 31 per cent of GDP, thus boosting the economy and leading to an overall fall in poverty levels, but for poor rural women the benefit, if any at all, was minimal.

This account of poverty in India and the complex array of changes that have occurred politically, socially and economically has left NGOs, and their work in the early twenty-first century, set in a context of uncertainty and challenge. The nature of poverty in India, and the changes in its structure that the economic reforms have brought, together with the related social changes, have amplified the difficulties that NGOs face. The opportunity for NGOs, therefore, lies in addressing the structural inhibitors that keep poverty levels high for the marginalized, including women. The focus then should be on those structures that deal with gender and powerlessness, but the dilemma is: how can this best be carried out?

Models of NGO intervention

As indicated earlier, the main model of intervention for the majority of Indian NGOs working in rural areas on issues of gender and poverty is the self-help group. It is a form of savings based microfinance, which is essentially a mutual-based model aimed primarily at women, and is now the preferred model for government, NGOs and multilateral agencies for community intervention in India. In 2006 there were over two million SHGs across India, with 33 million members and delivering services to well over 100 million people (Isern et al. 2007). The basis of the SHG is that 10 to 20 women come together to form a thrift and credit group: each member puts a small amount of money each week into a common fund, and after a period of six to twelve months, small loans from the fund are then made to selected members, based on their savings level and a needs assessment. This fund is often supplemented on a matching basis from additional resources from an NGO, either as a loan or grant, or by loans from commercial or state financial institutions facilitated by the NGO. These loans are then applied to a range of uses, which are ideally for productive purposes in that they will be able to generate additional income to enable repayments. They can also be made for necessary consumption purposes such as health costs and school fees, as well as daily expenses during an emergency or unemployment.

The model meets the demand of poor women for access to affordable credit, and it enables a broader social intermediation function by the NGO, fostering the notions of self-help and self-reliance that should lead to sustainability (Banerjee 2004). However, there is an argument that when credit is promoted, the financial accountability requirements and the resources required lead to the social change objectives being given a lower priority:

> [SHG programmes] ... tend to instrumentalize women either to improve their income or assets without necessarily having the effect of improving their status or access to resources/income. Women take up economic programmes such as micro-enterprise and increase their economic contribution to the household, without actually experiencing a corresponding increase in their social status or decision-making power at home.
>
> (Abbi 1999: 30)

The participation of women in SHGs is very much about the gender relationships within their households (for instance, whether the women's husband and/or extended families support or hinder participation in SHGs) and the social relationships and structures within the group, both of which, if not well managed, can add to the women's burdens (Ahmed et al. 2001; Kantor 2003; Murthy 2004). But not only is the potential burden on women an issue, these programmes tend to be discriminatory against the landless as they tend to favour people with some assets, usually land. NGOs tend to avoid these difficult issues, and promote the SHG model of microfinance as being relatively unproblematic.

Despite this 'downside' of the microfinance based SHG programmes, the evidence does suggest these programmes do reach the poor, and even though there is strong finance emphasis, empowerment outcomes are often achieved (Kilby 2006; Tesoriero 2005) – these outcomes will be examined in more detail in Chapter 5. At a practical level, microfinance-based programmes are a very important entry point for any form of social transformation, as very poor women do not usually have the time to come together at the behest of an NGO unless there is a clear tangible benefit to them and their families. Without the lever of microfinance through these savings programmes, NGO access to poor and vulnerable women would be much harder. The question, however, is whether microfinance displaces the social change work NGOs seek to achieve.

NGOs, self-help groups and empowerment

The features of the Indian NGO sector in the early 2000s presented in Chapter 1 present both challenges and opportunities for more effective community development programming and empowerment. For example, tighter regulation, promotion of SHGs, greater decentralization to local-level government, all led by the national government, have resulted in a sharp growth in the numbers of local or district-based NGOs. These NGOs are not only service providers, but are also facilitators of local-level activism and local-level power politics, and have a role as empowerment agents (Sen, S. 1999; Anand 2002). It is because these local NGOs are less visible than their national-level counterparts that they are able to take on some of the more sensitive advocacy roles, albeit at a local level. The dilemmas that the new local NGOs are facing, however, with the shift in their funding to more national and state government sources, is how to manage the balance between being efficient and effective service providers of government programmes supporting the local-level state, and supporting issues of empowerment, which requires flexibility and time, and some distance from the state.

These local-level NGOs would argue that they are able to meet their social change objectives such as empowerment *through* service delivery (Karlekar 2004). However, it can be also be argued that a service delivery approach leads to a relatively simplistic interpretation of the term 'empowerment', avoiding any analysis of the power relations inherent in the term (Lingam 1998). The SHG approach is also driven by a suspicious state, one which prefers to see NGOs confined to service delivery roles rather than empowerment, to which the controlling state is generally averse. Against state suspicion of empowerment programmes, both NGO and official international donors are aware that effective poverty alleviation requires, at the bare minimum, the participation of beneficiaries in development activities, rather than their being passive recipients. How far local NGOs can go in this fluid context is difficult to determine. For example, if we examine health care, an area which SHGs with group savings and local advocacy should be able to support, the evidence is that they have not been able to do much due to the hierarchical nature of health care provision in India, and the lack of health care facilities and service to start with (Nayar et al. 2004; Thorp et al. 2005). While there is little evidence to date, it would seem the use of SHGs in service delivery is not a viable solution, as they require an effective state around them to which they can advocate change. There are exceptions of course, as we will see with the case of Jagruti in Chapter 3. The other issue is that the groups themselves are not necessarily equitable and fair social structures, and most will have some barriers to entry, thus often excluding the very poor. This is not to say SHGs are not important and effective, but it is easy to overstate the real and potential benefits that they can deliver (Moyle et al. 2006; Thorp et al. 2005). Despite these limitations, however, international donors take the view that effective poverty alleviation requires that empowerment itself is a key component, and one that must go beyond mere service provision. However, the expanding role of the state as donor, through its government instrumentalities, does not see empowerment in quite the same light.

While the Indian state has effectively kept NGOs out of many of the broader political debates, at the local level there are greater opportunities for NGOs to use modes of intervention that enable both service delivery and empowerment, largely free of state scrutiny. As a consequence of the pressures placed on NGOs by the State through the 1980s, NGOs are now reluctant to act as spokespeople for the poor, but act more as mediators or facilitators to enable the poor and marginalized to speak for themselves. This has its advantages, as NGOs are generally not good in the role of spokesperson: they can exacerbate, rather than help overcome, the exclusion of the poor from the political processes. They can foster a level of dependency of the poor on NGOs to carry out the role of speaking for the community, rather than the more empowering role of facilitating the community to speak for itself (Kothari 1987; Robinson 1995). Despite the move to local NGOs and their role in encouraging communities to speak for themselves, there is still a danger of co-option, especially when local level NGOs engage with the state at any level. The other problem is that the reach of local NGOs is very small and fragmented, and local NGOs can also be compromised by more local-level state scrutiny, funding and political interference. On the other hand, smaller local NGOs may be able to more directly address issues of rights and political empowerment (Handy and Kasam 2006).

The discussion of the pressures that Indian NGOs have been under for the past 20 years highlights the point that for many the values base of social change for NGOs has been threatened by the imperative for survival and income. On the one hand, the move to smaller local-level NGOs provides an opportunity for the flexibility for effective empowerment programmes with stronger accountability links to the aid recipients, but on the other hand the pressures from local- and national-level governments and donors can place limits on this process. Given these complex forces that local NGOs face if they are to use SHGs for empowerment, how does this work in practice?

Empowerment

The growing popularity of the term 'empowerment' has led to a broadening of the definition to the extent that the concept is becoming less clear and is shifting away from the central notion of power, from which it derives. Some authors argue that the use of the term has become ubiquitous to the point that it seems to have become another buzzword in development practice, merely to repackage old aid programmes for the purpose of obtaining funding (Batliwala 2007; Cornwall and Brock 2005; Moore 2001). Development agencies often use the term 'empowerment' to refer to a range of activities, many of which have little to do with addressing the power relations among the various actors or groups in society, with the term often being used to:

> screen off power relations from the public discourse and obscure hegemonic relations. ... This conception of power as post-modern warm fuzzy expansible, not only conceals its hard edge; this cloak of opacity also discourages nasty questions of who benefits and how, and runs the danger of collapsing objectives, processes and outcomes alike into undifferentiated rhetorical empowerment.
>
> (Cheater 1999: 7)

In order to avoid generalized usage of the term empowerment, let us go back to the fundamental notion of empowerment and its relationship with power relations. As a starting point, I will propose a relatively narrow definition of empowerment: as being related to 'agency', or the expansion of individuals' choices and actions, primarily in relation to others. This definition of empowerment is important, as it can provide a basis for the measurement of empowerment; while at the same time being the foundation for broader social change, which entails access to power by those who are disempowered. It can be both a 'means' and an 'end' in the development process and is the key reason for its popularity as a development concept (Ackerson and Harrison 2000). As a 'means', the empowerment of beneficiaries in a development programme can lead to particular outcomes such as the improved management of community resources like schools and irrigation facilities to ensure their sustainability. Empowerment can also be an 'end' in a development intervention, in that the purpose of a programme may be the empowerment of a particular group of people who would otherwise remain disempowered – empowerment of women being probably the most common in this category. Such activities are seen as important in that empowered people are able to participate in development programmes, assert their rights and be in a better position to demand services from government and other service providers.

It is important to note at this point that empowerment is related to but distinct from 'participation' (another buzzword in development), when talking about changes in the relations of groups and individuals with each other and external agents. 'Empowerment' looks at participation in terms of expanded choices and action in community life, while the notion of participation is very broad and encompasses actions ranging from the mere provision of information, consultation, through to local control and partnerships (see Arnstein's [1969] ladder of participation). By focusing on empowerment we can move to greater local control and the processes required to achieve it. In this way the social relations between the beneficiaries of a development programme and the authorities should change. An essential aspect to empowerment is that an accountability relationship is also established between the patron (in development a government or a donor) and the client, so that a particular activity is sustainable and an ongoing flow of benefits is assured. So how do development interventions lead to empowerment outcomes, and what is the role of accountability in these interventions?

Theories of empowerment

The debate around the notion of empowerment in social relations can be divided into two broad views: one is that empowerment is primarily about the individual and changes in their cognitive processes; or the other, that empowerment is about changes in social relations. The supporters of individually-based notions of empowerment argue that it is only indirectly related to the direct exercise of power, but rather it is more about personal cognition and awareness from which other changes follow, and so this view eschews notions of domination, consent and resistance, in terms of personal changes: '[Empowerment] ... is a construct that links individual strengths and competencies, natural helping systems, and proactive behaviours to matters of social policy and social change' (Zimmerman and Rappaport 1988: 726).

Critics argue that those views of individual empowerment which avoid notions of control in favour of non-adversarial and relatively benign changes merely promote a *'sense* of empowerment' [emphasis added], that is cognitively based, a sense of personal control rather than actual control (Riger 1993). This distinction reflects psychology's two views of human nature: cognition, in which 'the person creates reality'; and behaviourism, which posits that 'reality creates the person', i.e. people are influenced by their environment. Riger's argument goes that it does not reflect an increase in actual power but rather is a 'false consciousness' (p. 281). The other more radical view of empowerment is that it is inextricably linked to political issues and rights, whether they are in the realm of patriarchy and the family, or community power structures (Kabeer 2005). Here empowerment entails a process of change for the powerless or disempowered, whereby these disempowering institutional structures are challenged. In this framework empowerment is not a passive process.

These two views of empowerment, while being placed at different ends of a spectrum, are not mutually exclusive. For example, there is the notion of both a 'performative aspect and a substantive aspect of *voice*' [original emphasis] in empowerment (Goetz 2001: 35). That is, empowerment has both cognitive *and* political components: it is not only a sense of having expanded choice but also of being able to act on those choices; and considers new forms of social identity, consciousness and cognition in human action (Mayoux 2000; Puroshothaman 1998). Empowerment has both cognitive and political dimensions: one cannot act without awareness, and similarly, awareness without corresponding action is meaningless. According to Jandhyala empowerment is:

> ... a process whose outcomes would lead to renegotiations of gender relations, enhance women's access and control over human, material, financial and intellectual resources, legitimize women's entry into non-traditional spaces, create new spaces, and support systems to sustain the process of empowerment.
>
> (1998: 205)

To tease out the debate on empowerment, a useful starting point is to examine the notion of empowerment at an individual level and then look at the implications and tensions that arise for the broader collective and political dimensions.

Individual dimensions of empowerment

The community psychology literature emerging from studies of alienation views empowerment as part of the building of an individual's self-knowledge and self-esteem to reduce feelings of alienation and enhance feelings of solidarity and legitimacy (Robinson-Pant 2004). Individual empowerment is 'the reciprocal influences and confluence of macro and micro level forces that impact the emotional cognitive and behavioural aspects of individuals' (Speer 2000: 52), and these changes are in:

- meaning which revolves around beliefs, values and behaviours;
- competence or self-efficacy, or the belief of being able to conduct particular tasks or roles;
- self-determination or the choices individuals have in initiating or regulating their actions;
- impact or the degree to which one influences the outcomes of others; and
- how people understand and relate to their social environment and the role of collectives in community life.

This approach, which is based on individual changes, does not acknowledge the structural issues which lead to empowerment programmes in the first place; for example, women's experience of disempowerment by virtue of the patriarchal structures in the family, and society more broadly. Therefore, another way of looking at empowerment is through the lens of *dis*empowerment: a 'lack of control over destiny' (Campbell and Jovchelovitch 2000: 261); 'polluting' events which are 'not fair'; an 'affront to dignity' (Kane and Montgomery 1998: 266); and 'isolation in decision-making' (Puroshothaman 1998: 50). What these views of empowerment and disempowerment have in common is a strong individual dimension, but it is these same disempowering factors, largely driven by social structures, that affect group dynamics and disempower whole groups. However, making a judgement on what is disempowering, and the structural drivers, can raise its own set of problems: for example, a perceived lack of control over destiny may simply be due to laziness, incompetence, individual preference, or different priorities; rather than the action of others, or structural inequality.

There are also differences between the various capacities of decision-making, that is different levels of disempowerment, and the different choices people make – people may simply choose not to choose. For example, a woman might be living in *purdah* (seclusion) because she is pressured by patriarchal or other forms of social power, or because she perceives there are benefits for doing so, such as gaining prestige, or maintaining her privacy. *Purdah* per se is not an indicator, but rather it is the socio-political context in which it is placed that determines the freedom a woman has to exercise her choice (Kabeer 1999). Demonstrating a causal relationship in these complex social systems is almost impossible. Kabeer argues that if disempowerment is to be meaningful there must be a 'deep-seated constraint on the ability to choose' (p. 438). This point brings us back to the structural issues I touched on earlier, which are related to power.

The complex relationships between empowerment and disempowerment, and the role of the individual and the group can really only be persuasively examined through the lens of power, and the related theories around power. A key theory by Lukes (1974) and others (Bachrach and Barantz 1970) is that the exercise of power is, in part, a constraint on decision-making: power is asserted by confining another's decision-making spaces. It is, more often than not, done subtly through manipulation rather than domination, and decision-making is restricted to relatively 'safe' issues, involving 'non decision-making' as much as decision-making. The exercise of power is less about conflict and more about influencing, shaping and even determining the wants of another. These nuanced approaches to the notions of power give some insight as to both why disempowerment is experienced, and the key characteristics of individual empowerment outlined above. In other words, people's lack of control over their destiny or inability to choose can be explained by the constraints on their decision-making space, and it is the overcoming of these constraints that is empowering. In this schema, individual empowerment then takes on different forms with different people: 'Depending on the context, empowering behaviours might range from individuals adjusting to adverse conditions that are not malleable to change, to working with others in a voluntary organization to alter the distribution of community resources' (Speer 2000: 52).

In summary, these views of empowerment are related to an individual's relations with others. Empowerment is expressed in terms of cognitive changes that in turn may lead to further actions in their relationships. This nuanced individualistic view of power, however, understates the broader political dimensions of power and the notion of domination (Riger 1993). An individual approach to empowerment is somewhat reductionist, and focuses too much on a sense of empowerment rather than on actual empowerment. The focus on the personal (in terms of how individuals feel or perceive the world) disconnects human behaviour from the larger socio-political context, and therefore serves to maintain a status quo rather than lead to substantial change. There are larger systemic issues that create powerlessness and negative life outcomes for individuals. The emphasis on personal empowerment also gives insufficient weight to the importance of co-operation among individuals and community processes: individual empowerment is more concerned with control than co-operation, while community empowerment is to some extent about subverting the notion of individual control to the community good (Riger 1993). It is possible to have an empowering collectivity that disempowers individuals and vice versa (Kane and Montgomery 1998). Empowerment, though, is not about simple trade-offs between the individual and the group: it is more about how the group can reinforce individual agency and vice versa. Individual empowerment can only occur in a social context and so must involve co-operation.

To bring the two competing streams together, a third analysis is to see power as enhancing the capacity to act rather than being about domination of others. Power through this lens is, by its nature, transformative and can be seen as an 'agent's capabilities to reaching outcomes' (Giddens 1979: 88). In other words, while power is usually directed at others, that is not the primary reason: power is asserted to give a particular benefit to those who exercise it, therefore power relations are two-way: 'however subordinate an actor may be in social relationships the very fact of their involvement in that relationship gives him or her a certain amount of power over the other' (p. 6). According to Giddens (1979) the subordinates in any power relationship are adept at converting the resources they have in terms of knowledge or social relations (or even physical assets) into a source of control, and therefore they gain some power. This can only be done if power has a collective character; it is a 'network of decision-making and an institutional phenomena' requiring a collectivity of support and an institutional framework in which to act (p. 89). The exercise of power is then a social phenomenon: 'Power within social systems, which enjoy some continuity over time and space, presumes regularized relations of autonomy and dependence between actors and collectivities in contexts of social interaction' (Giddens 1984: 16).

Power is the capacity of one or more agents to make a difference and influence change in others, and at the same time it is a structural resource of a community. Individuals can draw on power 'in the course of their interaction with others' as it is inherent in all social systems (Hindess 1996: 9). The implication then is that power is the property and resource of a social community, and thus involves reproducing relations of both autonomy and dependency in social interactions. This notion of power as a social resource with collective aspects, and being dynamic and multi-directional, brings us to the notion of agency.

Agency has two features: first, it is the range of choices that an individual might have (Kabeer 1999); and second, it is the capacity to exercise those choices, or to act on them. For Giddens, agency is a defining feature of being human: 'to be a human being is to be a purposive agent which both has reason for actions and can elaborate on them' (1984: 3); but agency is more than simple choice and action:

> Agency is about more than observable action; it also encompasses the meaning, motivation and purpose which individuals bring to their activity ... it can take the form of bargaining and negotiation, deception and manipulation, subversion and resistance as well as more intangible, cognitive processes of reflection and analysis. It can be exercised by individuals as well as by collectives.
>
> (Kabeer 1999: 438)

Agency can also be seen as a 'continuous flow of conduct' and so by its nature is an intervention (Giddens 1979: 55) and a 'continuous process by which action transforms both structures and individuals' (Giddens 1984: 14). In this theory, it has a feedback loop: the more one exercises their choices the greater the expansion of opportunities. The concept of agency and action is therefore tied to that of transformative power – it enables a capability to reach outcomes, and is a process of change. One way of looking at it, is as a continuum of conduct that can be divided into categories or typologies of power. For example: *power over*, which is about control and domination; *power to*, which is about the opportunity to act more freely within some realms; and *power from*, which is about the ability to resist the power of others (Hollander and Offermann 1990). In practice there is often a blurring of the understanding of the notion *power over* and *power to* in what is being sought in empowerment. Many interventions can increase people's power to act (their agency), by enhancing self-esteem, but do little to affect their power over resources, policies or, in the case of women, the patriarchy (Riger 1993).

The exercise of power is also related to the arenas or contexts in which it is used. Power is not only related to a capability to reach certain outcomes, but more importantly, it is related to access to certain domains and the ability to mobilize resources in those domains – 'domains of power' (Vijayalakshmi 2001: 4), or even access new spaces (Jandhyala 1998). These might be, inter alia: the household; the local institutional structures; the political community; the broader economy; and civil society. Power being seen as access to decision-making spaces, in the forms of various socio-political domains, is important for how NGO empowerment programmes may be conducted. It this understanding of the nature of empowerment, and the inherent tensions touched on above, that drives effective empowerment programmes. It affects the approach taken and the indicators used to determine positive empowerment outcomes either at the level of the individual or the group. However, it is also the collective dimensions of empowerment that are an integral part of the equation and cannot be ignored.

Collective dimensions of empowerment

Collective empowerment is in part how individual empowerment can affect collective processes (Pilsuk et al. 1996). At a superficial level collective empowerment is a summation of individual empowerment, which leads to the self-efficacy of a group: it is a collective phenomenon derived from the psychological empowerment of individuals. However, it is much more than this, as there is also strength derived from the 'web of continuing relationship ... [and] mutual support' (Pilsuk et al. 1996: 17), resulting in enhanced access by individuals to resources in the arenas of economic, political and social decision-making. The group gives voice, value, identity and support to the individual, and a sense of power develops in the course of collective action, which 'validates the primacy of ... agency and renders it more visible' (Puroshothaman 1998: 155. There is thus a feedback loop or virtuous circle: of personal power producing a collective sense of legitimacy and an awareness of a collective sense of rights (leading to collective action), which in turn leads to enhanced personal power. The outcomes of community empowerment, therefore, are a raised level of psychological empowerment, political action and a redistribution of resources and/or decision-making (Calman 1992). Riger (1993) argues that this process may not be so benign when a vicious circle emerges of individual or psychological empowerment undermining or weakening community empowerment as people begin to act more autonomously: 'The image of the empowered person ... reflects the belief in separation, individuation, and individual mastery ... [contrasts] with an alternate vision that emphasizes relatedness and interdependence as central values of human experience' (Riger: 285). The situations that foster communal or collective values are in tension with those that foster agency or control, that is 'control rather than communion' (p. 285). An individual's understanding of power and social change in a group, may differ from their own sense of control and efficacy. They may experience personal dimensions of empowerment, quite differently and in a disconnected way to how they see communal notions of empowerment. This tension lies between a person's instrumental values,which are attempts to control, and their expressive values, which are about interpersonal relationships.

Riger goes on to argue that expressive values, being about interrelationships and dependency, may be valued less in society than instrumental values, which are about control and achievements. However, the powerless, who are not in a position to exercise autonomy and choice, depend on communal goals to survive:

Does empowerment of disenfranchised people and groups simultaneously bring about a greater sense of community and strengthen the ties that hold our society together, or does it promote certain individuals or groups at the expense of others, increasing competitiveness and lack of cohesion?.

(p. 291)

Related to this question is whether the group is the means by which the individual is empowered, or is an empowered individual a way for a group to more ably assert its rights and needs? At a practical level these two questions raise the important issue of what is an appropriate balance between the personal and the collective in empowering processes, and how NGOs and others that seek to facilitate the empowerment of the poor can find this balance in the approaches they take.

Empowerment and development

The preceding section has argued that empowerment is about both groups and individuals, being group processes that lead to change in the lives of individuals:

> In order to be truly empowered, poor people must be able to go beyond their consciousness of themselves as eternal victims, to transcend their self-perception towards greater control over their lives and environment. This internal change in awareness, while catalysed by group processes, is profoundly and intensely personal and individual.
>
> (Sen, G. 1997: 5)

Not only do the group or collective processes provide a support or catalyst role for individual empowerment, these processes also provide a context through which individuals can become aware of the local realities, and in India the SHG can provide this role. This awareness occurs through the social cohesion the group brings, and the local networks to which the group exposes its members. For this process to occur, both individual and collective notions of empowerment must co-exist and prioritize the importance of control over resources. Control over external resources can give capacity for self-expression, while a change in personal agency can overcome barriers to accessing resources. Empowerment may be the balance between individuals accessing resources and their inner transformation. In India, it is a lack of understanding of this complex process that results in problems in both NGO and government empowerment programmes. Government programmes can falter because they focus on control over external resources, while NGO programmes can falter because they focus predominantly on inner transformations.

Empowerment also involves changes in power relations, which in turn can lead to some degree of social upheaval. At times, for example in gender programmes challenging patriarchy, empowerment is a zero-sum game with some (men) surrendering power while others (women) gain power. Empowerment is also related to the idea of development as 'a process of change in social dynamics [which] alters the social economic and political power base [and is] a process of confrontation'

(Gorain 1993: 381). While changes in power relations between societal actors may not always be a consequence of empowerment, a central tenet of empowerment is the potential and opportunity for these changes to occur. Empowerment, therefore, goes beyond the individual and the group, and enters the realm of political change and social justice. Empowerment then becomes more than merely choices, but a sense of personal control or influence, and a concern with actual social influence, political power and legal rights. This normative analysis should be treated with some caution, as it tends to gloss over the tensions between personal and collective empowerment outlined above. It risks romanticizing empowerment by ignoring the realities of power relations within groups and communities as a result of the intersectionalities of ethnicity, class, gender and other social divisions.

If we look at the rationale of development interventions for empowerment, particularly women's empowerment in a developing country context, there are three paradigms:

i An *economic* paradigm that promotes development interventions to improve women's capacity for increasing their income either through employment or micro-enterprises. This paradigm assumes 'reinforcing spirals' that occur as a result of increased income and economic independence, which in turn lead to social and political change and greater personal empowerment;

ii A *poverty alleviation* paradigm which focuses on decreased vulnerability and looks at 'mutually synergistic interests' at the household level. It takes the view that addressing practical needs, such as health or education, is the best way of addressing gender inequality and as a consequence women are empowered; and

iii A *feminist* paradigm, which addresses gender subordination at the individual, organizational, and macro levels. Economic programmes are seen only as an entry point for wider social, political and legal empowerment.

(Mayoux 1999)

These three paradigms are not mutually exclusive, but uneasily co-exist to varying degrees in development programmes, with women's empowerment as an assumed outcome in all three. The first two, the economic and poverty alleviation paradigms of empowerment rest on two assumptions: first, that there is an economic priority in people's lives; and secondly, that economic and physical well-being results in socio-political benefits through the increased choices that these benefits can bring. The problem is that these two assumptions are flawed: 'bringing women together for savings and credit does not necessarily develop a sense of solidarity or joint exploration of ways in which women's problems can be overcome (Mayoux 1999: 976). Likewise other microfinance studies that focused on poverty as being related to a lack of entitlements found that microfinance did not expand women's choices but in fact increased women's burdens (Goetz and Gupta 1996; Kabeer 2001; Mayoux 2001; Rahman 1999). In these cases women generally are held responsible by the facilitating NGO for the loans, but it is their male relatives who have the control. The women's workload is increased due to pressure placed on them from both within the families and from the NGO staff. These programmes have a paradoxical effect of reducing the choices available to women by adding to their burdens, creating dependency relationships with the NGO microfinance provider, as well as reinforcing gender inequality.

Economic programmes may not accord directly with women's immediate priorities. When women were asked to rank their own indicators of empowerment according to their importance in their lives, economic change was rated lower than education for children (Kilby 2006). The weakness of the economic and poverty paradigms is that they rest on general assumptions about the most appropriate path to women's empowerment and that physical or economic resource constraints are the reason for disempowerment. They do not recognize that for women, gendered power relations have to change in order to bring about changes in economic relations. The economic paradigm is dependent on a rather narrow social construct that describes women as economic beings, rather than social and political beings:

> The view that poor women only organize around economic issues in a passive and defensive way denies them agency and consciousness and misunderstands that the struggle itself can be a politically transformative process.
>
> (Hirschman 1998: 231)

Empowerment for women is more than them gaining the ability to undertake activities; it is also the capacity to set their own agendas and change events. Empowerment involves women in an active role, not only in decision-making, but also an understanding of the factors that shape a situation and the nature of oppression itself. Empowerment entails a transformation of social relations, particularly gender relations and processes; and goes beyond choices to obtaining access to new spaces, and social transformation. These views also point to a notion of empowerment that is 'iterative, non-linear and perhaps never complete' (Murthy 2001: 351).

It can be argued that one of the new spaces that empowered people should gain access to is the relationship with the patron NGO that may be facilitating empowerment. It is, in part, the accountability structure (to the people it is working with) of an organization that directly affects the people's capacity for empowerment. The further away the institutional structure is from a direct representation by its constituency, the poorer the outcome is in terms of empowerment. This then has implications for the models of development adopted by Indian NGOs and the approaches they take.

Conclusion

The issue that emerges, which is central to NGO effectiveness and the role of self-help groups, is how these disparate elements touched on in this chapter come together. The key element that needs to be examined is how the empowering potential of SHGs pans out at the ground level for women. The empowerment theory that has been examined points to a delicate balance that is required between the individual and the group, in how group dynamics influence effectiveness.

Hence the role of the NGO, and how it works with self-help groups, becomes important. At this level the role of government and its relations with NGOs is far less important, but nevertheless dominates NGO discourse.

The self-help group model certainly offers a potential for achieving strong empowerment outcomes in which the group provides both the catalyst and support for strong individual empowerment outcomes; but also, as we have seen, this is a delicate balance of managing power relations and enabling equitable and fair outcomes for the group. This is where the purpose of the NGOs comes into play, and as we have found the SHG model may be good for some things but not for others. The major focus recently has been on microfinance with a range of papers and reports focusing on the efficiency of SHGs as financial intermediaries rather then as empowering structures. The competing ideology is that greater financial security will lead to women's empowerment, against the competing view that expanding a woman's range of choices through self-help group activity can enable her and her group to not only expand economic activities but also demand better services from government and NGOs. The more challenging question is whether the level of empowerment possible through the SHG can advance gender relations.

3   Rural NGOs

Introduction

This chapter explores the changes that have happened to Indian NGOs in the early 2000s in more detail, using the examples from a group of mostly small local NGOs from Karnataka in southern India. Karnataka was chosen as it has a relatively benign social and political environment for NGOs to undertake their work. In the 1980s and 1990s when these NGOs were established, the benign environment provided them with more choices in the approaches they could take in their work and constrained them less than if they were working in other parts of India. Karnataka has also experienced rapid economic and social change over the 1990s and 2000s, which has provided both opportunities and challenges for NGOs. In what seems to be a paradox, since the mid 2000s the economic and social changes are now having a more negative effect on NGO capacity, in that they have given the government the resources to provide both more funding to NGOs. This funding, however, has conditions attached to it that both narrow and restrict the choices NGOs previously enjoyed when they were largely funded from abroad. This change will be examined in some detail in this chapter.

A total of 15 NGOs were surveyed, having being chosen for their focus being broadly defined as women's empowerment, with their aid recipients being largely made up of women. These 15 NGOs were from Karnataka and Maharashtra (See Map 1). Eight of these NGOs from Karnataka were chosen as case studies and will be looked at in more detail in this chapter. NGOs from two rural districts were chosen: the relatively poor district of Dharwad in the North, and Kolar in the south of the state close to the capital city and major technology hub of Bangalore. An NGO from Pune in Maharashtra the adjoining state, is also looked at in Chapter 4, by way of providing an urban contrast, as well as an interesting model against which to make comparisons. Karnataka also provides an interesting case study of NGOs in the twenty-first century, which are probably undertaking the most radical changes since Indian independence, with the rapid withdrawal of foreign donor funding for NGOs being replaced by government, both federal and state, funded programmes to assist rural communities.

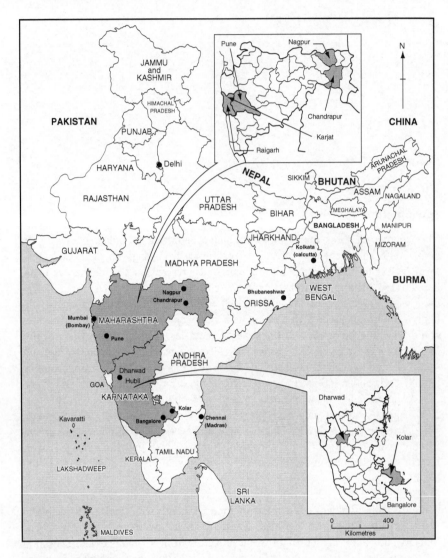

Map 1 Map of India

Resourcing NGOs

In the early 2000s the government support of NGOs had stabilized at a strong level by the consolidation of NGO regulation with fewer legislative or regulatory changes for NGOs to deal with than earlier expected, and in 2007 with the first national NGO policy in India (Planning-Commission 2007). There was, however, an attempt to introduce a new FCRA Bill in 2006 into the Indian Parliaments as detailed in Chapter 1, aimed at restricting NGOs' activities further by limiting their capacity to cost recover any of their work such as training programmes, having assets revert to the state in certain circumstances, and tightening reporting arrangements (Jalali 2008). While this Bill ultimately lapsed, the debate around the Bill, the NGO policy, and rapid growth in NGOs schemes supported by government, all signalled a greater engagement in NGOs and NGO work by government at all levels.

The real changes for NGOs, however, have been at the local NGO level, especially in southern India. There are two main interrelated drivers of this change. First is the sharp drop in international funding of secular NGOs in the mid-2000s; and second, the marked increase in state funding of NGOs from all levels of government. Another, but less important change had been a rapid increase in microcredit being sponsored by the state and provided through self-help groups (these have been traditionally more savings- rather than credit-based) and the role that some NGOs have played in this. The driver for these changes had been the rapid economic growth experienced by the Indian economy, especially in the southern states including Karnataka from the late 1990s into the 2000s, which provided government with the wherewithal to increase social spending, and NGOs were an obvious channel.

As a result of this shift in funding sources, from international sources to Indian government sources for many NGOs, their strategies had also changed. This change involved a winding back of many NGO activities and by 2009, many of the medium-sized district or sub-district based NGOs were unable to fully replace their international donor funding with government resources due to more restrictive requirements. As a result, in 2009 many NGOs were much smaller, many with half the staff numbers they had at the beginning of the decade. The reason for this sharp drop in funding was two-fold: first, smaller district-based NGOs had weaker capacity to manage government funding, which had a set of reporting requirements and institutional dynamics quite different to most INGO donors; and second, the Indian government bureaucracy, at both state and national level, was seen to be a more hostile environment than other donors, something that many NGOs had trouble dealing with. Other NGOs felt that to be true to their values and avoid going down the government funding path, they had to adopt some innovative practices, and formed new partnership arrangements, in order to remain effective. Examples of these will be looked at later in this chapter.

International development funding of secular NGOs in India had a steady increase until 2000, after which two events had an important impact. The first was the decision of the Indian government to sever relationships with most of their bilateral and multilateral donors in 2003; and the second was the Indian Ocean tsunami at the end of 2004. Both events were in the context of a booming Indian economy, with poverty rates generally falling and an improved government service delivery at local level, compared to twenty years earlier. For example, access to education had improved markedly, with female literacy rates increasing in the 1990s at twice the rate they did in the 1980s, and the gap between girls' and boys' literacy levels was slowly closing, with the strongest and most rapid improvement occurring in the southern states (Premi 2002). The response of many donors, both the official donors still in India and INGOs, in the first instance was to move out of southern India to those states where poverty was more intractable, such as Orissa and Bihar, and other pockets of serious poverty in northern and eastern India.

The enforced withdrawal of many bilateral donors, together with a very strong economy, sent a message to INGOs that India, and in particular southern India, was no longer a priority, and that the government itself now had the capacity to seriously address the country's social problems. On top of this came the Indian Ocean tsunami, which badly affected the south-east coastal states of India; and while the government took the lead in the recovery effort many INGOs effectively diverted resources from one part of India to work with local NGOs and others in the tsunami affected areas. An analysis of the foreign contributions to local NGOs reported to the Ministry of Home Affairs show that in 2003 the increase in INGO flows was only 1 per cent, representing a decline in INGO funding in real terms; while in the tsunami recovery period 2005–2007 flows to NGOs rose by 23 per cent, 26 per cent and 56 per cent respectively with Tamil Nadu being the largest recipient (Das 2005). Foreign donors also moved to a much sharper sectoral approach to funding, and in southern India this has been away from livelihoods and supporting SHGs as such, and more to funding HIV/AIDS, natural resource management, anti-trafficking and the like. There have also been much larger contributions to larger religious NGOs as the fears around Hindu fundamentalism have lead to concerns of the safety of Christians and the followers of other minority religions in India (Jalali 2008). The result was that long-standing smaller secular NGOs either had to change their focus to meet donor (in this case mainly government) needs or seek other sources of funding.

While international funding of secular NGOs had fallen, Indian government funding for NGO work in rural areas went up (Kudva 2005). There were a large number of schemes run from different government departments, dealing with welfare and development issues. Notwithstanding the difficulty in accurately measuring the level of this funding, Tandon (2002) had estimated that funding sources for NGO work in India in the early 2000s were roughly split equally between foreign donors and Indian government. On top of this the estimated value of private donations and volunteering (often overlooked) was equal to the sum of government and foreign contributions combined, giving a total outlay for development work at the time of Rs 16,000 crore or $US3.5b. Since those figures were compiled there had been further expansion in government programmes. For example, one government agency, the Council for Advancement of People's Action and Rural Technology (CAPART) expanded its funding of NGOs from Rs 54crore ($US12m) going to 4000 NGOs in the ten years from inception up to 1994, to Rs 300crore ($US67m) going to 10,000 NGOs in the following ten years, with an annual spend of around Rs 50crore (US$8m) in 2008 (Kudva 2008: 132).

The reasons for the increase in government funding can be explained by the fact that Indian governments rise and fall on the rural vote, which has both the largest proportion of the voting population and the greatest turn-out at elections. In this context, welfare and development programmes targeting rural areas have had strong electoral appeal. The problem, however, is that the government does not have the staffing and other logistical infrastructure to reach people effectively in rural areas, which existing NGOs have; thus NGOs are seen by the government to be a viable alternative for delivering services. From the NGOs' experience, though, these government programmes can have very high transaction costs, very low flexibility and high expected expenditure or 'throughput' rates. These funding requirements affect targeting the very poor as it takes longer to run programmes with this group due to the natural capacity constraints the poor have, in terms both of less time to participate in these programmes due to their existing long working hours and family commitments, and their generally poor education levels. These factors lead to a reluctance of many district-based NGOs to be involved in these government programmes.

Indian governments have also been involved in the other main NGO preserve, of promoting microfinance: resulting in a rapid rise in the number of self-help groups (up to one million SHGs in 2005); but more importantly, a shift in focus away from being a vehicle for family savings, to becoming a means of distributing credit to rural areas. That is, the SHGs have shifted from having a strong social or empowerment role, to having a more instrumental role of increasing credit availability. This is something that could have had an effect on empowerment outcomes, a point that will be returned to in later chapters. As a consequence of this and the downturn in traditional sources of funding, some NGOs had taken on the role of microfinance agents of one sort or another, as a means for them to survive. The implication of the increase in government programmes, and specifically in microfinance, is that there was a drift away from the very poor as the target group, towards the wider community more broadly. As with other programmes, the transaction cost for microfinance programmes to reach the very poor was high, outcomes were slower to be realized, the absorptive capacity was low leading to smaller loan sizes, and there was a greater risk of default. Given the political need to put more funds to rural areas and show some effect, it was natural for both government and their associated NGO programmes to shift away from the very poor as their target group. This was quite different to INGO funded programmes, which had a mandate to work more or less directly with the very poor.

A number of issues arise in this new relationship. The first is a definitional one, and that is who NGOs are and what their relationship is with other key community groups such as the Panchati Raj Institutions (PRI), the constitutionally mandated village representative groups as part of the governance structures of the village and sub-district (Fernandez 2004). On the one hand NGOs have a role in promoting these groups, and on the other they compete with them for resources. Likewise, the central government views have shifted in this regard; where earlier the Official Five Year Plans of the 1990s emphasized the role of NGOs, the later plans of the 2000s brought both the PRIs and NGOs into the picture, competing with each other for funding. At the same time some government agencies were also setting up their own statutory bodies with a quasi-NGO status (Fernandez 2004), or supporting the larger urban-based NGOs, thus:

> ... creating additional cleavages in the [NGO] sector, deepening the divisions between nationally and globally linked NGOs ... and the smaller NGOs of the districts ... [driven by] the 'competence culture' of the newer more directed and managerial focused NGOs.

> (Kudva 2008: 140)

NGOs and multilateral programmes

Multilateral donors such as the World Bank have programmes that are funded to, and administered by, governments but use NGOs as the conduit for implementation at local level. While these types of programme were not as common as other forms of government funding, they could be quite large and had their own unique characteristics, and NGOs' experience with many of them was particularly problematic. The main multilateral programmes that involved NGOs in Karnataka were World Bank programmes in rural areas, the World Bank Drinking Water Project, and the World Bank and DANIDA supported Karnataka Watershed Development Project (KWDP). The KWDP experience in Karnataka is a useful case of the issue of using NGOs as a conduit for government programmes as it affected most of the case study NGOs examined later in this chapter.

The Karnataka Watershed Development Project (KWDP)

The Karnataka Watershed Development Project (KWDP), known locally as Sujala, ran from 2001–2009, and was implemented in seven districts of Karnataka at cost of $US79m of which $US4.1m was funded through NGOs to develop SHGs. The project covered 516,000 hectares of land spread over 77 sub-watersheds, 1270 villages benefiting nearly 400,000 households. The project objective was to improve the productive potential of selected watersheds and their associated natural resource base. It is also to strengthen community and institutional arrangements, promote participatory involvement of primary stakeholders/beneficiaries and offer assistance to women, landless and other vulnerable groups by supporting investments in income generation activities to accelerate their entry and expand their participation (Milne 2007; World Bank 2009).

There were 53 NGOs used as implementing partners, responsible for the local community mobilizing of SHGs and also ensuring that some of the local infrastructure work was completed on schedule. This work typically involved arranging community meetings to agree on work plans and most importantly the payment of labour costs to communities on the completion of work. Given that the project, though ostensibly participatory, was planned with very tight output schedules and plans, for which NGOs were paid against (World Bank 2009), these NGOs were under much pressure to meet targets and provide detailed reports on output. The project also had an accelerated implementation schedule between each of the three phases over the life of the project. As the volume of work expected to be undertaken increased with the second phase of the project, tensions emerged with the Karnataka government, who felt that they should have closer control of the process. The result was a dispute in which many of the NGOs were not reimbursed for the work undertaken. For some this was up to a year while they covered the staff costs pending reimbursement. In 2009 many of the 53 NGOs were still owed money for the staff and other costs they had incurred. While the World Bank saw the performance-based contracting system as a success (World Bank 2009), the local NGOs were the main losers.

The reason for the dispute, which had adversely affected many NGOs, can be explained in terms of the institutional politics of these loan projects whereby funds are lent to the central government, which are then lent on to the state government. As these projects are loan projects for a social or environmental purpose, and will not generate direct revenue that can be used to repay the loans themselves, the government has to find the funds for repayment from other sources. As there is no financial benefit, the incentive then is for the government to gain political capital from these projects in the form of control and prestige. This, however, may not accord with sustainability and equity goals underpinning the projects, or most importantly, having NGO involvement in them (Fernandez 2004). NGOs, many of whom had a tradition of community consultation and longer-term approaches, could therefore be put under pressure from either the World Bank or the government to meet unrealistic expenditure and output targets that have limited outcomes, certainly in the short term, with poorer communities. For example, in the KWDP, while the original objective was for 70 per cent of the beneficiaries to be poor and marginal farmers, at project completion the figure was less than half that (World Bank 2009). These poorly planned donor requirements created conflict for the NGOs concerned, particularly with their values and the aid recipients, and ultimately it soured the relationships NGOs had, both with the World Bank and the partner governments.

The effect of these fundamental institutional changes being faced by Indian NGOs was that their role changed from that of being development organizations supported by INGOs with a more hands-off approach, to being social welfare agents for the government where the NGOs were expected to be implementers of government programmes on more or less a fee-for-service basis with high levels of government control (Baruah 2007). While the demands of INGOs to some extent involved compromises or small shifts in local NGOs' values, the domestic government programmes presented much greater challenges. While there were still opportunities for local activities and rights-based work or work aimed at the very poor, the resourcing of these programmes required a greater level of innovation and skills that was beyond the capacity of many local NGOs.

NGO responses

This very rapid change in the funding climate and institutional support base for Indian NGOs had a marked impact upon them, particularly those in the more prosperous southern states. As international donor funding dried up for secular NGO development work, local NGOs had to shed large numbers of staff and look to new ways of maintaining their impact and effectiveness with fewer staff and resources. Alternatively, they could have taken government contracts and maintained their effectiveness that way. There were essentially three options for Indian NGOs:

- 'downsize' and revert to the smaller more voluntary structures they had before international donor funding, and take on more modest activities at local level;

- strengthen their capacity, particularly financial and management, to be able to take on larger government contracts and to be discerning with those they take;
- to have independent sources of income through commercial or semi-commercial enterprises, such as undertaking consultancies or being microfinance brokers.

Of course, many NGOs adopted a mix of all three strategies. This chapter examines the NGO cases from Karnataka, looks at these changes and at how a group of NGOs in Kolar and Dharwad districts adapted.

Karnataka

Karnataka, located in southern India, in 2005 had a population of 53 million and, along with its neighbouring states, is where most of the dynamic growth of India is located. There had been substantial changes in the social indicators for India as a whole, and Karnataka and Southern India in particular, since the 1990s. The figure for poverty in 2005 for Karnataka was 25 per cent, which was below the national average of 27.5 per cent, and the poverty level for rural areas was 21 per cent (Planning Commission 2007a). This level of poverty represented a sharp fall from a high of 30 per cent in the mid 1990s (Census Commissioner 2002; Chelliah and Sudarshan 1999). This shift in the level of poverty also represented a shift in the poverty demographic from rural areas to urban areas. It should be noted, though, that the urban poverty line was at the time 65 per cent higher than the rural poverty line, and there was some debate about the relevant price movements and calculation of the indices that were used to validate that result (Murgai et al. 2003). Regardless of these debates, two-thirds of the population were in rural areas and this was where most of the poor were until the early 2000s.

The sharp fall in the poverty levels can, however, hide higher levels of poverty among certain groups in rural areas, and a relatively high level of inequality and depth of poverty across the state. For example, the income level of the average poor person was a full 8 per cent below the poverty line, a statistic that points to a high level of marginalization and poor prospects of many of the poor that were coming out of poverty, without focused interventions (Directorate of Economics and Statistics 2009). *Dalits* and agricultural labourers were the largest groups of rural poor, and represented 25 per cent of the poor in rural areas. The poverty figure for *dalits* in rural Karnataka showed the effect of marginalization and caste, with poverty levels for *dalits* being around double those of the general population when their share of the overall population was taken into account. On top of this 20 per cent of the rural population did not have access to safe water, and 54 per cent of children were undernourished (Chelliah and Sudarshan 1999; Das 2005; Filmer et al. 1998; PRIA 2009).

Women in Karnataka, as in the rest of India, were significantly disadvantaged relative to men on any measure of poverty or marginalization. Women had a low workforce participation rate of 35 per cent (Das 2005) and were found largely in unskilled low-end jobs such as agricultural labour, where they constituted 60 per cent of the agricultural labour force, but only 30 per cent of cultivators (that is, being able to own the harvest either as a farmer or sharecropper) (Das 2005). In agriculture there had been a feminization of agricultural labour, with casual labour (mainly undertaken by women) rising from 39 per cent in 1994 to 45 per cent in 2000. The Indian government had for some time recognized that women were a particularly disadvantaged group and had been targeting them through government programmes since the 1970s and 1980s, focusing on the underlying causes of women's disadvantage (Viswanath 1993). Taking a lead from government at that time, NGOs also started to focus more on women's programmes, and in the 1980s and 1990s women's empowerment programmes sponsored and supported by NGOs emerged.

The NGO case studies

This section looks at the experience of eight NGOs from two districts of Karnataka and how they adapted to the rapid changes in the institutional context that small local NGOs were finding themselves in. These NGOs were generally district-based and tended to respond to the needs in those districts, though, in some cases, they operated in more than one district. The experience of these local NGOs was typical of many small NGOs found at district levels in India and how they adapted to rapid change.

Dharwad District, where four of the NGO case studies were working, lies in the north-west of the state, with a population of 1.6 million in 2001, of which 69 per cent were engaged in agriculture. It was drought prone with limited irrigation opportunities, leading to a precarious livelihood based on the vagaries of the weather (Census of India 2001). The position of women is this context was even more vulnerable as they made up 90 per cent of those workers in the District who were without secure employment, with the only job prospects being in agriculture in a marginal physical environment. The sex ratio for Dharwad was very low with only 948 females per 1,000 males (well below the state average of 964 (Tata Energy Research Institute 2001) and women's literacy level in the mid 1990s was only 24 per cent (Sharma 2006). The economic position of women in Dharwad District was at best marginal, and in response to the clear need NGOs had been involved in community-based development programmes for the poor and disadvantaged since the 1970s, with a rapid growth in the numbers of local NGOs since the early 1990s.

Kolar District lies immediately to the north-east of Bangalore in Southern Karnataka, with a population of 2.5 m people in 2005, and also drought prone, but here there was some tubewell and tank irrigation to compensate the dry environment. Around three-quarters of the population work in agriculture, and as in Dharwad, there were few work opportunities outside of agriculture for women; even though Bangalore was close by, it is more difficult for women to move there for work due to the prevailing social mores. The sex ratio for Kolar was 970 in

2001, well above the state and national average, but this was probably explained by men moving to nearby Bangalore for work and leaving the women back home. For most villages, clean water supply was inadequate, and only 16 per cent of the population had access to medical care as less than one-tenth of villages had a health clinic. Only 25 per cent of villages had public transport access (Directorate of Economics and Statistics 2009). Kolar district also had a reputation for political divisions even at village level, which made changes like the Panchayat Raj Act, and even social services through NGOs, difficult to implement.

The NGOs

In this part of India it is the district-based NGOs that were the primary contact with local communities, first emerging in the 1970s, but with a rapid increase in numbers in the 1980s and 1990s. These smaller NGOs had generally replaced the Gandhian organizations of the 1950s and 1960s, which were then the main NGOs at district level. In Karnataka, most district NGOs usually formed themselves into loose networks for communications and developing relations with government. In Dharwad District, for example, there was an NGO Council with some twenty members, but only half of these NGOs were active at the time of the survey. The women's self-help group (SHG) model had been the main mode of operation among development NGOs in Karnataka, partly because it was widely understood and seen to be successful; and partly because it was actively promoted by both central and state government, with many government sponsored community development programmes at the time being predicated on NGOs adopting a self-help group model for community organizing. Since the early 2000s, some government agencies have begun to take on an NGO form, in that many of their programmes use the SHG model, and the intersection of NGOs and these government programmes have led to common models and approaches (CARE 2009). Major multilateral development initiatives also use local NGOs as a major conduit, with a popular model being to use a larger nodal NGO with strong management and administrative capacity as a channel for supporting a number of smaller local NGOs, which have strong links to the community.

Chinyard

Chinyard (Chaitanya Institute for Youth and Rural Development) was established in 1990 and by 2008 it was working with 2537 active SHGs with 48,000 members (CARE 2009), with 200–300 new groups being added each year. In the 1990s the support for Chinyard's establishment came first from another local NGO, Indian Development Service, and then the Hyderabad office of an INGO with offices in India provided funding to support Chinyard being reorganized and registered under the FCRA to receive foreign funds. Despite the success of its earlier work, Chinyard had to deal with a number of institutional setbacks in the early 2000s, which are to do with the problem that many small locally based NGOs have, and that is their dependency on one funding source for their core costs and the high level of vulnerability this can bring. In this case the sole INGO funder ceased funding Chinyard in 2000 as a result of a policy to move its work to concentrate on the poorer northern states of India. This left Chinyard having to seek other supporters. The effect on the staff was devastating, with staff numbers falling from a high of 30 permanent staff in 2000 to seven in 2005, as the organization struggled with one-off support from donors over many years, as well as involvement in the Karnataka Watershed Development Project and the institutional vulnerability that brought. It was not until Chinyard met the requirements for microfinance accreditation in 2007 that staff numbers were able to increase, to the point when there were 25 staff in 2009.

As a result of Chinyard's loss of international donors to support its work, from 2000 it adopted a strategy of increasing its microfinance work and diversifying its funding sources. In 2002 Chinyard became a partner in the KWDP, with its role project being to expand its SHG programme and engage them in specific income-generation and watershed management activities. At the peak of the Project work there were 40 staff working for Chinyard, but due to the change in policy of the Karnataka government in working with NGOs and its failure to reimburse the programme after the change, the programme collapsed as far as NGOs were concerned, and Chinyard was still owed Rs 800,000 (US$20,000) in 2009. As a result Chinyard accelerated its application for microfinance registration and was registered as a microfinance institution in 2007. This enabled it to lend to self-help groups as an agent to the State Bank of India, which was different from its previous work where it facilitated the links with banks rather than act as an agent for them. The advantage of registration was that it was able to increase the scale of the work considerably, and receive a commission for managing the loans. The loan disbursement rates for Chinyard managed funds grew quite quickly, going from Rs 395,000 (US$8,000) in 2006 when they had only provisional accreditation, to Rs 3.2m (US$64,000) in 2008 when they were fully accredited. By 2009 they had agreements to manage more than Rs 20m (US$0.4m) over three years from the State Bank of India, and were expected to receive over time a further Rs 200m (US$4m) from the Department of Women and Children to lend for micro-enterprise projects for women.

For the SHG programme, the criteria Chinyard had for recipients of the microfinance programme was for a strong poverty focus, with a requirement that SHG members be categorized as below the poverty line (BPL) in order to qualify for assistance. In 2009 Chinyard had lent to Rs 15m to 257 SHGs, with Rs 500,000 being repaid and a repayment rate of 95 per cent. While Chinyard had an established set of procedures for loan recovery, and up to 2009 this had worked quite well with none of its loan portfolio classed as 'at risk' in 2008 (CARE 2009), this type of operation still had considerable risks as any default had to be covered by the NGO. The margin that Chinyard receives to cover their operational costs from the Bank is 3 per cent on the loan with another 1 percent allowed as an administration fee. This represented a very tight margin for which even a 5 percent default rate would not be sustainable over time. In order to cover the institutional costs to transform itself into a microfinance institution, Chinyard received institutional support from a US Foundation focused on India that supported entrepreneurship.

Chinyard had also set up a number of village forest committees as a part of community-based management of natural resources and several vermi (worm based) compost units – as a part of its sustainable agriculture programme (Wiserearth 2005). They had also applied for support for a small-scale (irrigation) tank rehabilitation project where they hoped to be able to tap into the village SHG resources, to provide labour as a complement to their microfinance programme. Funding outside of the microfinance programme in 2009 came mainly from state and central government development funds. Despite the changes in funding sources, Chinyard tries to ensure that all its work conforms to its mission to:

> ... bring about sustainable development through self-help, with special emphasis on participatory conservation and management of natural resources, equity and gender sensitivity, [all with the central objective to] eradicate poverty and empower the masses, especially women.
>
> (Chinyard 1999: 1)

Up until the 2000s the work of Chinyard dealt primarily with microfinance and resource management, total health, violence against women and micro-enterprise development, with the largest programme by far being microfinance through the SHGs. The challenge it had for the future was that as external funding had dried up it had to secure a stable programme and avoid the institutional disruptions that occurred in the early 2000s, which saw it both losing its main donors and being involved in the rather insecure World Bank funded Karnataka Watershed Development Project. This period saw staff numbers rise and then fall very sharply, leading to a very insecure institutional environment. The other critical issue was the role a single donor can play in programme development and programme strategy for a small NGO. While there is a place for donors in having a strong dialogue and establishing joint priorities, the power relationship that funding brought at that time left Chinyard in a weak bargaining position, with the feeling that it had to take up the programmes of the donor.

India Development Service (IDS)

IDS, also located in Dharwad, was started in 1974 by non-resident Indians living in Chicago, USA to fundraise to support development work in India. In 1977 two members of IDS from Chicago, S. R. Hiremath and his wife Shyamala, visited India to identify suitable programme areas, with the intention of developing their own operations rather than funding other NGOs, which they had been doing up to that time. They decided that Dharwad would be suitable and settled there in 1979, registering IDS in India in the same year. Over the following twenty years they built up IDS into a strong local NGO, but then started to withdraw from the day-to-day operations in the late 1990s to take on predominantly a governance role. The goal of

IDS has remained a commitment to the economic and social development of India through the 'development of people'. In 2009 IDS had a highly committed and experienced staff complement of 43, somewhat down from the peak of 73 staff in 2004.

Like all of the NGOs in these case studies, IDS's work had changed quite a bit from 2000 to 2009, and to a large extent this reflected the changes in funding that had occurred to NGOs more generally in Karnataka. Up until 2002 the focus of IDS was on SHG development when they worked in 100 villages with around 500 women's self-help groups, targeting mainly landless labourers, artisans, and small and marginal farmers. IDS facilitated SHGs usually have 10–15 members, a little smaller than the 20 member average SHG that is promoted by government and other NGOs. With a smaller group size IDS found there was more opportunity for greater participation by all members. The SHGs were usually grouped in villages into what they call a Village Development Society, and these were in turn federated at sub-district level into Federations. IDS found, however, that these Village Development Societies require ongoing support, and IDS had to return to the original groups some years later to re-invigorate these SHGs and provide them with further institutional support. One of the reasons for this lack of sustainability may have been that IDS prefers to promote what it refers to as collective leadership among SHGs members rather than having the SHGs elect leaders from the outset. The intention was that over time natural leaders would emerge to take on an informal role of ensuring the groups were well led. The problem was that this did not happen to the extent hoped for. The IDS staff member was seen as having the role of catalyst, and as responsible for developing a 'sense of partnership' between the beneficiaries and IDS development workers. What happened in practice, which is common among NGOs supporting SHGs, is that a level of dependency emerged, with the NGO staff taking on a quasi-leadership role.

The work with SHGs was put into a difficult situation from 2002, as foreign funding dried up. IDS became more involved in government programmes, the most notable being the World Bank supported KWDP discussed above, where IDS was both an implementing agency and a nodal agency in two districts for a number of other NGOs. As seen earlier in this chapter, this programme was complex, and the demands by the donor and Karnataka government were such that the IDS as an agency was strained. By phase two of the programme, like many other NGOs involved in the Programme, IDS was unable to meet what were seen to be unrealistic demands in the rate of service delivery. There was a lot of infrastructure work involved in watershed management, as well as facilitating and monitoring the work to be undertaken. The expectations of the rate of work and the project expenditure rate were unrealistic, and IDS took the decision to pull out of the programme, with a substantial number of outstanding bills, leaving IDS with large debt. The other key issue with this project that drove the decision to withdraw, was that it moved IDS away from its focus on the poor and landless to those with land, who could implement and host watershed infrastructure (Hilemath 2004). As a result of this experience and the debt incurred from the KWDP, IDS had to scale back their work and in 2009 they were involved in a small number of relatively small discrete projects:

IDS projects 2008–2009

- Forest and bio-diversity programme with 173 village forest committees with each having five SHGs;
- A health and livelihoods programme supporting village health workers;
- Organic farming supported by the Department of Agriculture;
- Skill training programme for the poor funded by central government;
- Capacity building programme under the National Rural Employment Guarantee Scheme; and
- A small environment awareness programme to support local communities in their campaign to clean up a local factory whose expansion will lead to water contamination.

IDS had found that this new approach of being involved in a range of programmes which were, to varying degrees, directed by government presented a challenge, and so it was looking at ways of reconnecting with the SHG groups and associated federations as way of keeping the links with its values on a firmer footing. IDS had found that working with government had had some adverse effects, ranging from the programme target communities moving away from the poor, to the prosaic issue of being forced to have different categorizations of staff depending on whether they were working on government programmes or not (Hilemath 2004). This caused problems, as those working on government programmes were required to be paid at a different rate to IDS staff.

Despite these challenges, IDS maintained a strong commitment to its values and it saw the strengths of the programme as due, in part, to a dedicated staff, a low staff to group member ratio, smaller average group sizes, and an active policy of targeting the landless and those with low literacy levels. However, according to IDS' own analysis in the early 2000s, in one of its programme areas only around one-quarter of the groups were sustainable and had reached a strong measure of empowerment after three years, and nearly 20 per cent of groups were 'weak'. Following the loss of many of its external donors and the involvement in government programmes in the early 2000s, IDS lost touch with these groups, and in 2008 IDS was in the process of re-engaging with those groups through their federations to re-invigorate them.

Accountability to the aid recipients was a priority for IDS, reflected by the responsiveness of staff to community needs, the ambivalence to government funding and the policy of having some direct consultation of the Board with the groups. Likewise there was a strong degree of staff autonomy to be directly responsive to community needs and to react to their priorities in how they programmed and provided resources. Paradoxically, though, this fostered a high level of dependency of groups and the Federation on staff. This raised the issue of the right balance between providing support and fostering dependency. Despite these challenges, IDS had a strong institutional base to continue to be effective in empowering the poor and marginalized to engage with issues as they arose. The challenge was whether a level of individual empowerment could be translated into group autonomy at local level, which would strengthen the collective role of women in local political, social and economic life. The changes in the sources of support for NGOs in general, and IDS in particular, make this a difficult challenge.

Jagruti

Jagruti is an important case study as it is an entirely voluntary-based NGO with no funding at all, and belongs to that group of NGOs that represent, in sheer numbers at least, the largest category of development NGOs (Tandon 2002). Jagruti is a small NGO, which in 2001 had been working for around 10 years with a handful of volunteers organizing self-help groups in six villages with saving schemes and facilitating the local community to deal with local issues such as access to services. Being volunteer-based it had the challenge of finding ways to keep the volunteers engaged so they continued the work. So where it could Jagruti found funds from local foundations for its small number of paid staff from time to time for one-off activities, but by 2008 this funding had ceased. While the original approach of working with SHGs was moderately successful, it was not being resourced, and was little different to the work of larger NGOs in the district. As a result the management and Board of Jagruti decided in 2004 that there would be a change in direction, approach and focus, with a sharp move to more clearly rights-based programmes. The focus was on health rights and supporting people's claims for better health services and ensuring they were receiving what they were entitled to. Jagruti, with support from the Child Rights and You (CRY) Foundation, was able to work with 400 existing SHGs in 35 villages to train the members on their health rights, with a view to improving the practices at the Primary Health Care centres at sub-district level.

Jagruti and health rights

In some government run health clinics in Dharwad District, as in many parts of India, poor people were being charged for treatment when it is meant to be provided free of charge. In one case of direct action a community that had been supported by Jagruti held a series of protests at the clinic. The District Health Officer was petitioned by the people and Jagruti on a number of occasions to no avail. The community then took the decision to lock up the health centre and stop it operating. The threat of the Centre being unable to function forced the District Health Officer to act, and he removed the corrupt staff and improved the service.

The CRY supported programme came to an end in 2008, and left Jagruti with some dilemmas. Jagruti was a small voluntary agency with few resources and the challenge of where to allocate them. While Jagruti was quite effective in its work, it did sap the energy of the volunteer workers and the leadership. In 2009 the range of activities Jagruti was undertaking on a voluntary basis included: work against trafficking of young women – they had set up anti-trafficking committees in a number of villages; and promoting the Employment Guarantee Scheme in a number of villages, to ensure people were aware of it and could take up the work on offer if they needed to – Jagruti had prepared a booklet on this scheme.

While these activities were important, they were time-consuming for the volunteers, who felt they had to commit a large amount of their time to the organization. There was no international funding without FCRA and it was unlikely that FCRA would be approved, or if it was, that funds from INGOs would be available for such a small operation. On the other hand Jagruti was too small to take on government contracts, even if that was the direction a small voluntary organization like Jagruti wanted to go. This is an example of the dilemma that small voluntary NGOs have; and that is, while they are effective, unless they can scale up they are destined to fade away through the burnout of volunteers. It can be argued that it is these small volunteer groups that are central to the broader NGO fabric, and they are the source of many of the values that drive NGOs.

KIDS

KIDS (Karnataka Integrated Development Society) was a small NGO that was started in 1994 by a small group of concerned social work graduates with a particular concern for women and children, and it received full registration in 1997 (KIDS 2000a). In 2009, KIDS had 16 staff and its values were based on a commitment to women and children through promoting their social and economic 'upliftment' and empowerment in both urban and rural areas. KIDS does not have a specific poverty focus, but rather works with the socio-economically marginalized women who are vulnerable, such as sex workers, and trafficked women and children. Trafficking was and continues to be a problem in Karnataka, particularly from the poorer districts to major transport corridors and larger centres. The women were trafficked for prostitution, and the children for labour in hotels and restaurants. The target population for the self-help groups KIDS facilitated were women from backgrounds including migrant workers, scheduled castes, scheduled tribes, as well as widows and married girls, all of whom are vulnerable to trafficking. The focus was on the decision-making power of women and on reproductive rights, as well as socio-economic development.

KIDS provided services in family and HIV counselling, especially to sex workers and truck drivers; a child labour programme which involved advocacy on children's rights, as well as running special schools for child labourers; self-help groups for women; HIV/AIDS awareness raising; and awareness-raising among women on property, dowry and human rights. Also, KIDS had initiated a separate programme called Manavi which included a domestic violence hotline and legal support for women who were victims of violence (KIDS 2000b). Manavi had supported cases related to dowry, sexual harassment, property, domestic violence and rape. The child labour programme was among children in Dharwad who were engaged in waste-picking, and focused on their education, providing them access to schooling and a small stipend to partly reimburse their time away from work. KIDS had received support from the state Education Department to assist their work with school drop-outs. It was also involved in child labour advocacy such as bringing the attention of the authorities to the prevalence of child labour in local hotels. They facilitated a children's forum across 30 villages, where the children met every two weeks and discussed issues relevant to them; and from there issues went to a federation of children forums, which lobbied government on issues of child labour and child marriage.

KIDS also worked with around 300 SHGs to facilitate human rights awareness. In addition to this core work they had also received support from the Clinton Foundation to support children affected by HIV/AIDS with ARV treatment and counselling. They operated a women's counselling centre funded by the central government; and had a major campaign to raise public awareness against child marriage, and lobbied the state government to regulate the practice of mass marriages in Karnataka, where up to 15 per cent of brides may have been under age. For mass marriages KIDS lobbied the organizers of the weddings, and the state administrators, to ensure all brides had a state-sanctioned proof of age for marriage. They had also done work with *devidasi* (the traditional Hindu temple prostitutes) for the Anti-Slavery Foundation, with the aim of freeing them.

KIDS, like the other case study NGOs, had issues with the drop-off in donor funding but not to the same extent as the others. While KIDS programmes had continued without major cuts, their institutional support had always been precarious, based on a high turnover of both projects and donors. Like many agencies KIDS did not have regular donors, but depended on a number of different programmes to keep them going. KIDS' only independent funding came from the commissions they received from being an agent to provide insurance to poor women. Apart from that KIDS were not engaged in other commercial or income generation activities, as they felt it would take their time away from their programme work. KIDS was able to survive in this almost 'hand to mouth' fashion, as funding for child and gender rights short-term projects was generally forthcoming, but it was much harder to get longer-term institutional funding. This may be because funding agencies did not see children and women's rights as longer-term strategic issues in quite the same way they saw poverty and livelihoods.

Grama Vikas

Grama Vikas was a medium sized NGO based in Kolar district in Karnataka with a driving vision of social and economic empowerment focusing particularly on *dalit* women and children. Its goal was to empower marginalized rural women with stress on children and the environment, and network with Rural Women's Associations to accomplish sustainable development through food security (Grama Vikas 2000:1). It was established in 1980, following concern at the high levels of malnutrition among children in the area, highlighted by a governmental report released the year before. Grama Vikas' initial emphasis was a child development programme, however, this expanded into a women's empowerment programme relatively early on in the organization's life. As Grama Vikas took the view that development was possible only when women had an active role in development activities, however, a child development programme remained an important focus in the organization's work. The strategy of Grama Vikas in working with *dalit* communities in villages was initially through child development programmes by establishing *balwadis* or pre-schools. The approach of having an entry point through children overcame local tension between the higher caste community and *dalits*. After a level of village acceptance was reached with the *balwadi* programme, SHGs were developed with the most marginalized women in that community, most of whom sent their children to the *balwadi*. This slow and indirect approach through a children's programme was necessary as other NGOs encountered problems of access if they attempted to work directly with *dalit* or other marginalized families. The vast majority of Grama Vikas groups were made up of the *dalit* and tribal groups in the community.

The other key feature of Grama Vikas' approach was that the programme expanded at the rate of the capacity of the SHG to self-manage the programme, that is, they did not work to a timetable. There was a strong emphasis on self-management with Grama Vikas staff moving out of direct group management as soon as possible, but being in a position to provide support at all times. The management of the SHG programme was in the hands of two representative bodies: one that dealt with the children's programme and was made up of a parents' committee; and the other was the main representative body dealing with the women's empowerment programme – the Grameena Mahila Okutta, registered in 1997. These two bodies were responsible for the day-to-day running of the programmes, income generation (including dealing with donors), local-level advocacy, basic social sector work and SHG management. Gram Vikas was also involved in higher-level advocacy and managing some local environmental programmes. It also provided some secretariat support to the two representative bodies, broader strategic work as it related to community needs, and also in the strategic direction and support to the federations.

Grama Vikas has an all-women staff team apart from the General Secretary. This was seen as important for the effective organizing of groups. Of the 40 staff in 2005, around 15 were involved in working with the SHGs, with another three having an SHG audit role. The reason Grama Vikas had such a successful pro-gramme in employing women is that it provided secure live-in facilities with rooms attached to the *balwadis,* all within walking distance of the groups the women were working with. At these facilities a couple of women lived together and so provided support to each other. This strong reputation for catering for the safety and security of women staff, and an all-women team, made Grama Vikas an attractive place for young women to apply to work.

The vast majority of the women who worked for Grama Vikas were young and single so staff turnover was high. This was not seen as a problem and was even an advantage as the staff could not dominate the groups over time. This fostered self-reliance in the groups, with the staff having a supporting role. Gram Vikas was very clear in its empowerment policy and ensured the staff had values in common with the organization. There was a one year orientation programme, which involved regular training programmes and new staff being placed with more experienced staff for mentoring: this way the new staff member had to complete a form of apprenticeship.

In 2007 there were over 300 women's SHGs in over 167 villages, with more than half having reached a level of self-management that they can be linked directly with commercial banks. Grama Vikas' programme was committed not only to economic and social empowerment among marginalized women in Kolar District, but also to self-run institutions for the SHGs. The majority of the groups were sustainable and could largely manage their own revolving funds. One problem for Grama Vikas was that its programme was resource intense in that the women's groups were not only responsible for the SHG management, but had a role to play in other resource distribution to the village, e.g. having a role in managing the children's programmes. It was in part the threat of losing some of these resources (such as the children's programme) that focused the SHG leadership energy on resolving issues within the group, to avoid the group failing.

The success of this programme meant that it attracted further funding from donors and government to provide as credit to SHGs. An injection of large sums into groups through government or donor subsidized schemes, however, meant that the members' equity in the group could possibly drop from a high of, say 90 or 100 per cent, to as low as 10 per cent. There was the risk of problems with repayment rates, and given that even in the older groups not all members had accessed loans for capital, the groups themselves could have easily divided among themselves into a situation of 'haves' and 'have nots'. The risk here was that it could create conflict and fragmentation, and disempower some members within the SHGs. Grama Vikas managed these risks well and did not have the same drop in INGO support that the other NGOs this chapter covers had. It managed the changes in funding by maintaining long-term relationships with child sponsorship agencies, and had even expanded to the neighbouring Raichur district in 2007. The advantage of child sponsorship funding is that it does not use the projects cycle approach that other INGOs use with official back donors. This way Grama Vikas can secure its funding in the medium to longer term.

MYRADA

MYRADA is a large NGO aimed at social and economic empowerment. It operates in three states of southern India; Karnataka, Andhra Pradesh and Tamil Nadu. MYRADA's values were: justice, equity and mutual support for marginalized communities through 'fostering alternate systems of the poor through which they mobilize and manage the resources they need [through] institutions which form the basis for their sustained empowerment' (Fernandez 2004: 3). MYRADA began in 1968 and was the oldest and largest organization of the case studies. In its first decade it worked with Tibetan refugees in Karnataka but in 1979 moved into broader development work. In 2009 MYRADA worked in 12 districts across three states, with over 10,000SHGs (which MYRADA refers to as self-help affinity groups – SAGs). This figure included 500 sex worker groups and 400 watershed area groups. These were all women's groups with the exception of the small number of watershed groups, which had both men and women members (MYRADA 2009: 6). There was a staff complement of around 500. By 2009 MYRADA's donor profile had changed markedly, with around 70 per cent of their funding coming from Indian federal and state governments. While there was strong growth until the early 2000s, the two major INGO donors flagged that they would be withdrawing their programme from southern India in around 2010, and so from 2005 MYRADA began a planned change in its approach to its work.

Over a four-year period (2007–2010) the various programmes within MYRADA were set to become autonomous organizations within MYRADA, with a greater setting of direction by the local staff and aid recipients, with a view to them becoming independent NGOs in their own right. The mechanism for the devolution was through the Community Managed Resource Centres (CMRCs), of which there were 96 established in 2009. These CMRCs would continue to provide support to the SHGs as well as watershed associations and sex-worker groups, with each CMRC being responsible for around 100–120 SHGs (MYRADA 2009: 6). This more decentralized structure provided an opportunity for upward growth from the community organizations directly, but with the centres taking a greater role in accessing resources themselves. As the major source of resources was increasingly government funded programmes, MYRADA felt that it would be more successful and sustainable if the CMRCs directly accessed these programmes, as they were closer to the target communities, which some government pro-grammes preferred. In 2009 around one-third of the 96 CMRCs were in a position to cover their own costs with over half being able to cover 75 per cent (MYRADA 2009: 40). The CMRCs each had their own Board on which MYRADA had two nominees. The plan was for all of the CMRCs to become fully independent in the years following 2010, when the first eighteen CMRCs became independent NGOs. MYRADA saw itself as being no longer at the centre, but providing a mentoring role and the 'institution' of last resort for the CMRCs (Fernandez 2004).

Following these changes MYRADA began to focus its work on more strategic issues, and on engaging with government. In 2009 it was working with village governments to improve their administrative capacity for the programmes they implemented. It undertook training and capacity building for NGOs and SHGs and *gram panchayats* (Village Government), and it was working with the central government to improve the management of government-run SHG programmes. It also assisted the Indian Planning Commission in developing district development plans in those districts where MYRADA had experience, but district administration lacked the capacity themselves. This shift of focus for MYRADA meant that it was still able to have influence and development impact, but from a much lower resource base that was derived from their independent sources of income, such as consultancies, and a corpus of funds that covered their head office expenses, rather than INGO donors.

Prakruthi

Prakruthi is a small organization aimed at social and economic empowerment working in Mulbagal Taluk in Kolar District in Karnataka. It had its origins as a small village group within Grama Vikas 1982, but as it grew in size and influence it slowly developed its own identity until it reached a stage where it could be independent . Prakruthi was also an intermediate service organization supporting 35 other NGOs in Karnataka Tamil Nadu and Kerala on behalf of a local network of former partners funded by a major INGO in the early 2000s. Prakruthi worked in 70 villages with 150 women's SHGs covering some 2,200 families. As well as the SHG programme, Prakruthi was involved in a natural resource management programme, child development, health, and strengthening village assemblies. It saw itself as a non-political body in the civil society. The values of the organization were based on the premise that 'sustainable development can only take place in the context of an organized committed groups or society', with a mission

> ... to develop and support the process of an ongoing struggle of the disadvantaged section of society and help them find their own ways and means of alternative sustainable development strategies which can be applicable affordable and can bring measurable collective improvement in their life condition.
> (Prakruthi n.d.)

Like the other NGOs mentioned in this study, from 2005 Prakruthi had the challenge of a sharp drop-off in donor funding, when the last international donor ended its support in 2009. Prakruthi was also involved in the KWDP programme and as with the NGOs in Dharwad, the changes in policy within the programme saw Prakruthi not being reimbursed for one year's expenditure that it incurred as part of that programme. As a result of the issues with KWDP and the move of INGO donors away from Karnataka there has been no expansion, and Prakruthi had to cut back their staff from a peak of 73 people in 2004, to 33 by 2010.

Overall Prakruthi had a programme committed to economic and social empowerment among marginalized women in Kolar District; however, one of the schemes that was being considered by Prakruthi was a government-supported microfinance scheme that would see an injection of Rs 150,000 into each SHG and also provide a fee to be able to cover some of Prakruthi's costs. As for IDS, the challenge for Prakruthi was that the members' equity in the group would drop from 90 or 100 per cent to a mere 10 per cent, leading to the problem of insufficient attention being given to addressing social issues in the group and fostering an atmosphere for empowerment. The danger was that this could cause problems with repayment rates and a feeling of reduced ownership, which could in a worse case disempower the groups. As with the similar microfinance programme taken up by Chinyard there are quite a lot of risks for the organization as it goes forward, both in terms of maintaining values and being viable. Of the organizations in this set of case studies Prakruthi has been the most affected by both the loss of INGO donors and the issues of the debt from KWDP. In 2009 there was no clear plan to manage the funding issues.

RORES

RORES (Reorganisation of Rural Economy and Society) was a small NGO aimed at social and economic empowerment, that worked in Kolar District, but also had a small programme across the border in Chittoor district in Andhra Pradesh. It started in 1989–90 but spent the first three years establishing itself and making contact with local communities. Initially it worked in 15 villages, but through the 1990s RORES expanded its programme reach to 60 villages. From this work in the 1990s a federation of SHGs facilitated by RORES supported the SHGs, and by 2009 it was largely independent. In the early 2000s RORES had a number of separate programmes, such as a watershed programme supported by the Andhra Pradesh government in Chittoor district in AP; a government of Karnataka State Women's Development Corporation supported programme, with 40 villages; and the Integrated Sustainable Development programme working in 60 villages in Srinavasapura taluk (sub-district of 500 villages) supported by a number of INGOs. RORES was also involved in the KWDP but did not incur losses as many of the other NGOs did.

Since 2005 most of these programmes had been wound back as INGOs with-drew, and the fall in INGO donor funding had seen the RORES programme reduce so that in 2009 it was involved with only 146 SHGs, and this number was unlikely to change. Their staff numbers had fallen from a high of 30 people in 2005, to 12 in 2009. In 2009 RORES was involved in a school lunch programme, a horticulture programme funded by the state Department of Forestry, and organic farming projects supported by the state Department of Agriculture. Most importantly, however, was that RORES had become more strategic in its approach, with their most important programme being an information campaign in one taluk on the Right to Information Act. Under the Right to Information Act all levels of government – federal, state and local – had to provide information on government programmes if requested. RORES published a bi-monthly broadsheet newsletter with details of government programmes available and their details. The newsletter included information on: infrastructure projects, such as the winning of tenders and their details; the school lunch programme, to which schools, and what was included; and the welfare programmes including the ration shops, the food that was available and details of which ration shops had their scales certified by the Weights and Measures Board. Making this information more widely available ensured that people knew their entitlements, and at the same time made it harder for providers to skim off benefits for themselves, or engage in corruption. RORES managed and implemented this programme with only one staff member, and the information provided had a direct and ongoing benefit to these communities, especially the marginalized.

The other issue was the sustainability of RORES as an organization. In 2009 it was reducing its presence in the core programme area, and at the same time it was also engaging in income generation activities through the production of *spirolum,* a dietary supplement made of processed blue-green algae, which it marketed through its NGO network. It was also supported by funding generated from the executive director's commercial microfinance programme for the middle class that operated in local urban areas. The profits these commercial activities generated were sufficient to support the Right to Information newsletter and covered the core costs of the organization. The strategy of RORES, to overcome the drop in funding, was to develop independent commercial sources of income and take on only a few government programmes. This has enabled it to continue some of its core programmes, and ensured that it was able to have a major focus on the marginalized in the district. The cost was a narrower focus of their programme.

Conclusion

This chapter has looked at the rapidly changing circumstances in two districts in Karnataka, and how NGOs have responded to the changes brought about by rapid economic development, and as a result the withdrawal of many INGO donors from the Karnataka. The focus has mainly been on the smaller NGOs and the strategies they have adopted to survive. Three points have emerged: the first is that level of poverty and marginalization in Karnataka was still serious in the poorer districts, despite the rapid economic gains made at the state level; the second is that the NGOs in the case study had all continued their work, but with serious disruption and restructuring required; and third, they adopted a range of different strategies for survival. These strategies ranged from expanding commercial operations to provide core support, in the case of RORES; splitting off local operations so that they can better access state resources, as was the case with MYRADA; operating a microfinance operation as was the case with Chinyard; to establishing new long-term donor linkages, which Grama Vikas undertook.

While there was no uniform solution to the challenges, it was the resilience and ingenuity of these local NGOs that saw them through periods of rapid change and uncertainties. The other key feature of the experience of these local NGOs was the role of INGOs, and also multilateral donors such as the World Bank. While it was expected that INGOs and their funders would pull out of economically successful states such as Karnataka to put their limited resources in areas of greatest need in the north of India, it was the process of withdrawal that is worth examining. With the exception of the MYRADA donors, there did not seem to be a process of withdrawal and adjustment from the donor over a longer time frame. Given the extent of the work for many of these NGOs and the communities they reach, a three to five year process of withdrawal would seem reasonable. Related to this were the management processes of the World Bank KWDP, where the Bank saw the move to results-based contract management as a strength. In effect it resulted in the failure to reimburse the NGOs for work completed and effectively shut down some of the NGOs' ongoing programmes that were outside the scope of the KWDP. More work was required by the Bank and government agencies in their results-based management approaches as the search for quick results often left ineffective projects and reduced NGO infrastructure in their wake.

4 Pune waste-pickers programme

Introduction

This chapter looks at a programme which did not follow the traditional NGO model, but rather took a radical step in terms of the development approaches of an NGO working with marginalized communities. In this case it was an urban programme in the city of Pune in Maharashtra, the state immediately to the west of Karnataka, working with waste-pickers to support them to realize their rights. The radical difference was that from the very start, the model of intervention was that it was led by the aid recipients – the waste-pickers. Here the role of the local NGO, in this case the Centre for Continuing Education of the Women's University (SNDT), was akin to a service provider to the waste-pickers' own organization, the Kagad Kach Patra Kashtakari Panchayat (KKPKP) – from Marathi this translates as 'the association of waste-pickers in the city'.

Waste-pickers

So who are waste-pickers? In the streets of any large city in India you will see small groups of women (and sometimes children) around and inside garbage skips, sifting through and collecting scraps of paper, tin, plastic and cloth. These are the *rag pickers,* as traditionally they collected rags and bones, but this has broadened to include recyclable waste more generally, and so the more accurate name is waste-pickers. In India's pervasive caste system, waste-pickers sit fairly close to the bottom rung, being a sub-group of *dalits*, a name that in Marathi literally means 'suppressed' or 'crushed' – the most marginalized in society. The *dalits* were kept to the most menial and unpleasant tasks, such as cleaning up other people's rubbish, and other such jobs that higher caste Hindus would not do due to their degrading nature, being seen as 'unclean' in the Hindu religious tradition. This particular group of *dalits* came to Pune in 1972 from the rural areas of Maharashtra where they were agricultural labourers, following a devastating drought; and in Pune they found that waste-picking was about the only work that *dalit* women could do, outside of more poorly paid domestic service.

The programme that SNDT developed had its genesis in 1990 when it started an informal education programme for working children in the urban slums of Pune. It

---

Waste recycling in India

Informal waste recycling in India with minor regional variations has been structured in a pyramid form with scrap collectors or *rag-pickers* at the base, generally being women and children who access garbage dumps (landfill sites) and the large and small bins in the streets. Women do the more menial waste-picking work as men will not do it but work in the 'upper' end of the waste recycling pyramid. The male scrap collectors have push carts and buy scrap from small shops and businesses, and are also scrap collectors.

Thirty per cent of the women are widowed or deserted and over half are the major contributors to the household livelihood and less than 10 per cent are literate. They collect paper, plastic, metal, and glass scrap moving on foot 10–12 km per day with headloads as great as 40kg, and earn a little over a dollar a day. This scrap is sold to scrap dealers some of whom are registered, who are almost exclusively men who are in a position of power and frequently cheat the women through manipulating their scales or buying waste on credit and not paying on time.

---

was here that SNDT staff met child waste-pickers and accompanied them on 'their forays into garbage bins' and saw the lives they led (Chikaramane and Narayan 2005: 1). The informal education programme brought to SNDT the broader social justice and socio/political issues of slum life: key among these is the realization that income generation programmes did not reach the very poor, who have little time for additional income generation activities as they are mostly involved in very low paid, full-time and often labour-intensive work. The main issue waste-pickers had was less about their income levels, but more about changing the terms and conditions of the work they were doing as waste-pickers: a problem that waste-pickers have worldwide (Samson 2009). SNDT realized at the time that for a programme to reach the very poor it had to target working people as workers, and see waste-pickers in that light. 'it was clear to us … that there could be other claimants to the 'wealth in waste' and small group endeavours were not likely to counter the threat and this became the basis for organizing the waste-pickers on a mass scale' (Chikaramane and Narayan 2005: 2). The solution that SNDT and the waste-pickers came up with was to work with the waste-pickers as an organized group in mass actions around their rights, rather than adopt the more common NGO approach of treating the issue of marginalization as an individual livelihood issue. Over the next twenty years the waste-pickers of Pune, as an organized group, moved from being a marginalized and openly oppressed group in the city life of the early 1990s, to having a central role in the revamped waste collection system of the city ten years later.

Waste-pickers and SNDT

While as an occupation waste-picking is lucrative in comparison to the alternative opportunities *dalit* women have in cities, it is regarded as 'dirty' and the preserve of a 'lower' sub-caste of the *dalit* community, and mostly women and their children. While waste recycling is important for a whole host of reasons that are well known, up until the late 1990s it was not seen in that light in urban India. Waste-pickers were seen as 'scavengers', actively discriminated against, harassed by the police and government officials, and treated badly by scrap dealers, with the legitimacy of their work being continually brought into question. In 1990 SNDT was supported by an international organization to undertake an adult literacy programme with the children from the informal sector, including those of waste-pickers. After some initial work with the waste-pickers it became clear that there was little demand from the waste-pickers or their children for literacy, but rather the level of discrimination and official harassment made their work situation difficult, and at times quite tenuous. After the initial contact with SNDT the waste-pickers approached them as to what they could do to deal with their difficult working environment. The main issues they faced, as mentioned above, were not only dealing with putrefying and dangerous garbage, but also issues of discrimination including facing police round-ups when there was a theft in the neighbourhood, being cheated by the scrap traders they had to sell the scrap to, and the stigma associated with the occupation. The critical issue became one of establishing an alternative identity of waste-pickers as 'workers' rather than as 'scavengers'.

This led to a programme shift by SNDT, away from non-formal education towards what could be described as a rights-based approach that focused on the right of waste-pickers as *waste-pickers*, and the legitimacy and respect that should be associated with that role and identity. The second major shift was the realization that a traditional approach of a development agency in setting up a 'project' with a predetermined time frame, and a set of outputs and outcomes to address these complex issues would not work. As a result SNDT approached an INGO that had an office in Pune for an ongoing institutional support grant to work with waste-pickers with a relatively open-ended scope for the types of activity that would be under-taken. In practice the development approach adopted by SNDT became an iterative one where the implicit objectives and outcomes expected were continually chan-ging as the waste-pickers progressed in having their rights realized and issues addressed.

The philosophical approach of SNDT in the programme was from the outset, to first and foremost acknowledge waste-picking as a legitimate and worthwhile occupation, and that it should be supported as such, rather than having SNDT (or any other agency for that matter) seeking to provide programmes aimed at alternative income generation: 'to establish an alternate identity for waste-pickers as "workers" premised on the belief that scrap collection was socially relevant, economically productive and environmentally beneficial "work", and that working conditions could be changed' (Chikaramane and Narayan 2005: 3). The strategy then was to identify a process for formalizing waste-picking as a legitimate occupation, and the only viable way that SNDT and the women could see to do this was through a representative institutional structure. A trade union was the best model given the inherent political nature of the struggle that waste-pickers were engaged in. Such a trade union, however, would be different from an industrial union as the waste-pickers were self-employed, and did not have a formal association as employees with the municipal corporation, which governed Pune City and as such had responsibility for all waste management, including solid waste management (as garbage collection had come to be called). The union model was preferred over a co-operative structure, as the struggle of the women waste-pickers was primarily about their lack of recognition and dignity, in often de-humanizing conditions, rather than securing a share of an industry per se. But as we shall see in this chapter, a separate co-operative structure did emerge. A trade union structure also inherently recognized waste-pickers as 'workers' and enabled them to adopt the methods of trade unions in negotiation, and their assertion of rights. This included the strategic use of agitation methods such as rallies, demonstrations and sit-ins to demand change, as being important and legitimate means. This was not only to achieve their immediate ends, but also to assert their dignity and solidarity as women waste-pickers. While waste-picking as we have seen is highly gendered with little opportunity for women to enter the higher end of the waste recycling pyramid, having their rights respected is a major step, and was empowering in itself.

The leadership in the early years came from Dr Baba Adhav who at the time was President of the trade union of 'coolies' and 'head loaders'. He argued that a critical mass was required, and so a convention of waste-pickers was organized in 1993. Eight hundred waste-pickers attended from across the city, who one after the other recounted their stories of the indignity of their existence under a state of continual harassment. This convention led to the formation of the KKPKP) as a trade union which established the waste-pickers as 'workers' and so provided a framework to form a communications link between them and the municipal corporation. The KKPKP was formally registered later in 1993 with the 800 original members who attended the convention earlier that year. By the late 2009 KKPKP had a membership of 8000 waste-pickers, 90 per cent of whom were women, and around half were active in the union to varying degrees. It had a representative structure with an elected council of 95 women and 5 men who meet every month to determine priorities. It had as a central tenet the use of non-violent *satyagraha* resistance, to challenge systemic injustice to waste-pickers and their communities.

KKPKP: the early years

The key issue that the waste-pickers faced in the mid-1990s, as we have seen, was a lack of legitimacy, which in turn fed into a number of other hardships they faced in their day to day work. The lack of respect from their peers, and the community more generally, resulted in them seeing little future for themselves or their families outside of rag-picking, and so children were not sent to school but were often made to follow their mothers in their work of waste-picking, as well as other forms of child labour. This lack of self-respect and legitimacy led to low prices from scrap dealers, and official discrimination from the municipal corporation with their role being seen to be on the edge of the law, and subject to persecution as vagrants and 'scavengers'. SNDT took an approach to breaking the cycle of low self esteem and lack of legitimacy, that involved talking to the waste-pickers and sometimes work-ing with them at their workplaces. The SNDT staff came to understand the issues waste-pickers faced and identified with them. From these cautious initial steps membership of KKPKP was slowly built in the city wards, and from there repre-sentatives were selected. By 1996, as the numbers and confidence in the union grew, the union representatives were being elected from within each slum area. It was important for both SNDT and the union from the outset, that the representative nature of the union be accepted, and so formal meetings were held every month to discuss issues between the 100-strong council of waste-pickers and SNDT staff. KKPKP had a governing board of 11 members (eight women and three men) of whom eight were scrap collectors, the President was the son of a waste-picker and there were two non waste-picker activists associated with SNDT, also on the board.

The other important principle adopted by SNDT was that the organizers who worked with the waste-pickers have a close understanding of these women and their work, and so as part of the 'induction' for staff, they spent some time with the waste-pickers at their workplace and worked with them in picking out recyclable waste. There were four organizers originally employed for this role, with three activists in the role of broader management and strategic oversight. This meant that the organizational structure was small and able to avoid becoming too bureaucratic; and it also meant that a lot of the organizational work had to be done by the waste-pickers women themselves, thus instilling autonomy from an early stage of the organization development. From SNDT's point of view they offered and promised nothing in a way of tangible benefits or services, but rather a belief that collective action could end individual isolation and injustice (Mander 2002). There has also been a certain amount of goodwill for the waste-pickers' plight from the broader community who see their struggle as justified, and so the pejorative views of trade unions were avoided.

Identity cards

One step towards obtaining legitimacy and avoiding harassment was to establish legitimacy through a recognized identity for waste-pickers, and one that clearly classified scrap collection as legitimate work. While *rag-pickers* were recognized, and more often than not disparaged, as a caste identity, waste-picking as an occupation was not recognized in the same way. The solution that the union came up with was the idea of an identity card – the existing ration cards and the like established the women's identity as *dalits*, residents and welfare recipients, but they did not establish their identity as waste-pickers. The union, through a series of demonstrations and public rallies from 1993, lobbied the municipal corporation to provide, or at least recognize, an identity card for waste-pickers. In 1995 the Pune Municipal Corporation became the first municipality in India to recognize and endorse the identity cards issued through KKPKP to *authorize* the waste-pickers to collect scrap, thus recognizing their contribution to the 'work' of the municipality's waste management processes. This wording of 'authorize' was important as it was a much stronger terminology than 'allow'. It implied a right to the waste, rather than merely access to it under the grace and favour of the municipal corporation, and a result of the introduction of the identity card was that the level of harassment of KKPKP members fell markedly.

Cooperative scrap store

Scrap was big business and the waste-pickers salvaged 144 tonnes of scrap worth $3.7m annually in Pune in 2005; of this, the waste-picker earned a little over a dollar a day (Chikaramane and Narayan 2005), and so it was important that the waste-pickers received a fair price for their scrap. The price being offered by traders on any particular day was due to a number of factors, not least the globalization of the solid waste trade, where recycled paper and plastics from the west ended up in India for reprocessing, leading to a crash in local prices when a ship of recycled paper, plastic or metal arrived. Another factor, which was more easily controlled, was the monopoly that local scrap dealers had. The women waste-pickers had little bargaining power as they belonged to a marginalized group who were actively discriminated against when dealing with male scrap dealers and often received prices well below the going rate. The solution that the union came up with was to have their own co-operative scrap store as competition to the established scrap dealers. The union negotiated with the municipal corporation to get some space under one of the many 'flyovers' that were being built across the city where they could have a some space for a store. The co-operative scrap store was set up in 1998 as a wholesale buyer, which while only moving a very small proportion of the total waste collected, had the effect of providing some competition to the commercial wholesalers, and so placed the women in a stronger bargaining position. The co-operative scrap store provided an outlet if a reasonable price for scrap could not be reached. The 40 or so women who sold their scrap there every day were given a cup of tea and shared in the profits at the end of the year, half of which went into a provident fund and the other half was a cash dividend. The accumulated reserves from the store of Rs175,000 (US$3,500) enabled them to expand, and in the ten years since that first co-operative scrap store another three stores were opened across the city.

Savings and credit co-operative

As the poor generally describe their most important needs as jobs and credit, the next obvious step after securing waste-picking as an 'occupation' was to sort out the issue of credit. The waste-picker women were not only being discriminated against by the waste buyers, but also by credit providers to the point that they were not seen as credit-worthy. This forced them to depend on expensive money-lenders who charged around 5 per cent per month flat rate of interest to cover their credit needs. The women asked KKPKP if they could help. The approach the union took, rather than using existing microfinance approaches, which were less suited to urban environments, was to adopt a credit union model with a weekly collection of both saving and repayments from each slum area. The credit was originally for basic consumption items, but by 2009 there had been some move towards loans being provided for children's school fees and housing costs. In 2009 the credit union served 3,000 women and the union had an established relationship with a bank to provide an ongoing line of credit. The maximum loan was Rs50,000 ($US1,000) and the interest rate was 12 per cent per annum. A further six per cent went into a social security charge, to build a provident fund for the women. From 1999 interest free deposits from benefactors enabled KKPKP to build a corpus of Rs300,000 in funds to capitalize the credit union. Since then the credit union has declared a dividend of 10 per cent every year paid to the members after covering costs.

In 2002, as the credit union matured, they found there were still a significant number of waste-pickers who were not taking advantage of their service, simply because they were too poor to meet the savings requirement, and their income was too low and insecure for unsecured loans. The KKPKP undertook some research with this group and found that they were using the pawnbroking services offered by moneylenders, where they would be sold a small amount of gold to be used as collateral in a pawnbroking arrangement. The poor women would receive an ongoing line of credit secured up to 60 per cent by the value of the gold, but at the existing high interest rates. As a result of the study KKPK undertook a campaign against the moneylenders, and at the same time secured a fund of Rs200,000 through local well-wishers with which they redeemed the gold from the money lenders and took over any outstanding debts. KKPKP then set up their own pawnbroking service as part of the credit union, but offered a 2 per cent per month rate rather than the 5 per cent per month offered by money lenders. As a result of the credit union rates and the campaign, the moneylenders dropped their rates to match the credit union rates.

Later years: KKPKP autonomy

In the early 2000s, after the union had been operating for around 10 years, KKPKP began to look for ways to secure its independence from outside support by INGO donors and others. While it was appropriate to receive support for small one-off pilots or research activities, it was important that as a union KKPKP be self-funding for its institutional support. While union fees from such a marginalized group would never be enough to run the costs of a union, they were hoping they could build a corpus of funds so that the income from it would be able to cover the costs. The breakthrough came when after years of sustained lobbying the union had waste-picking in Pune classed as an 'unclean' occupation by the government (Chikaramane and Narayan 2005) and therefore eligible for an education subsidy. The Maharashtra Government approved the waste-pickers through their Municipal endorsed identity card to be classed as being engaged in an unclean occupation and so be eligible for the Pre-matric Scholarship for Children, which was subsidized on a one-for-one basis by the central government to give a total grant of Rs5000 (~US$100) per annum, per family (Ministry of Social Justice and Empowerment 2004). Until that time only the children of night soil carriers and similar workers were eligible. The campaign to broaden the classification to include waste-pickers was helped by a supportive media with headlines such as 'Government finds rag-picking too clean to merit help' (Chikaramane and Narayan 2005: 15).

This subsidy, which was only available to KKPKP members, resulted in a rapid increase in union membership. As the union played an important part in negotiating the classification and subsequent subsidy payments, there was a strong argument from the union leadership that new members should pay 'arrears' membership from the time the union was formed in the mid-1990s.

> They are benefiting because we struggled. For years without complaint we attended programmes, protests, marches, meeting and conferences. We did not calculate in terms of immediate benefits. All those years [other] women laughed at us. … Today they benefit because of our efforts. Let them pay for it.
> (Waste picker women quoted in Chikaramane and Narayan 2005: 29)

There were no complaints at having to pay the Rs350 ($US7 in instalments) for the fees in 'arrears'. This set of fees then made up a corpus fund so that from 2002, KKPKP no longer needed institutional support from external donors, being self-funded from fees and interest income. This education subsidy continued for four years, but by 2009 payments had been suspended on the grounds of high costs if implemented across the state, and so the campaign for waste-picker justice continued.

Health

Another important breakthrough as a result of ongoing campaigns by the KKPKP and its members was that Pune Municipal Corporation recognized the health risks inherent in working with solid waste and agreed to cover health insurance pre-miums from 2002. This was the first municipality in India to do so, and it was important as it confirmed the status of waste-pickers as a formal part of the waste management under the purview of the municipal corporation. Like every step of the way in fighting for waste-picker rights, it was not without its problems. For example, the insurance company objected to the large number of claims from waste-pickers and stopped paying out on many of the claims, even after the municipal corporation paid increased premiums. This dispute was only resolved following direct action through sit-ins by waste-pickers outside the insurance company offices, leading to the administration of the account being moved to another office of the company. KKPKP also looked at alternative health strate-gies including occupation health and safety by improving the tools-of-trade the waste-pickers use, including providing rubber boots, gloves and the like.

Education

The issue of accessing education for waste-pickers' children had been an issue for KKPKP since its inception, as the role of children in waste-picking was institutionalized to a large extent. In the early years 1989–1996, SNDT provided non-formal education classes for out of school children, which were supplemented by and then replaced with annual school enrolment drives. At the same time there was a focus on schools not to discriminate against waste-pickers' children (such as being sent home for having dirty/torn clothes and the like). 'They [waste-picker children] were the first to be shouted at and the last to receive text books and uniforms due to them from the Municipal school system' (Chikaramane and Narayan 2005: 19). Incentives were also provided for waste-picker children to go to school, with notebooks and prizes from KKPKP, and the Maharashtra state education system provided additional food rations to the families of those children with 80 per cent or higher attendance rates. This was in addition to the education subsidy for those classified as being in 'unclean' occupations outlined above. KKPKP also approached corporate sponsors to provide bursaries for higher education. While there was a requirement that members of the union do not use children for labour or engage in child marriage, ensuring access to education for waste-picker children was an ongoing issue for KKPKP since its inception. While there was a drop of 75 per cent in the incidence of child labour in waste-picking in 2005 due to the union's work, there are still children working as waste-pickers.

Solid waste collection and handling (SWaCH) co-operative

Since the late 1990s there has been a national move in India following a ruling from the Supreme Court to develop a national standard for Municipal Solid Waste Handling, with regulations coming into effect in 2000. Among other things, they directed municipalities to undertake measures for doorstep collection of waste, and its segregation in the household into various categories of recyclables – common in the West. The implication of this regulation was that the waste-pickers would be displaced if doorstep collection was privatized, something that occurred in the small city of Nasik in Maharashtra, where waste collection was done by private contractors, putting the local waste-pickers out of work. KKPKP also had a similar experience when residents in some wealthy areas hired private contractors to collect waste at the household doorstep, thus displacing 20 waste-pickers in one area. In another area, 300 waste-pickers negotiated for doorstep collection for 25,000 households, charging a nominal amount for the service, as well as the return from the waste collected (Mander 2002: 3640).

Given their earlier experience, this regulation posed an opportunity as much as a threat for the members of the KKPKP, provided that the waste-pickers could be integrated into doorstep collection. If this occurred they believed they would improve their working conditions, improve their earnings and 'transfer their status from scavenging to service provision' (Chikaramane and Narayan 2000: 16). While the Pune Municipal Corporation was slow in implementing doorstep collection on a large-scale, due to resistance from both the municipal workers unions and the waste-pickers union (albeit for different reasons) KKPKP saw the inevitability of the move and became proactive. They put to the municipal corporation that

KKPKP would conduct a trial across seven wards of the city to see if doorstep collection by waste-pickers was feasible on a large scale. This trial commenced in 2005 and after eighteen months 1500 waste-pickers were reaching 150,000 households, being 30 per cent of the city. Given this success the waste-pickers argued that they should be given the contract to cover the city (Express Newservice Nov 2, 2007). The trial did raise a number of issues: for example, the waste-picker women did not like being paid monthly; the households did not like to be paying for a service they thought they paid their rates paid for; and the Corporation also had reservations. But none of these problems were insurmountable, and in the end they were all resolved.

After some intense negotiations, further studies, and some backsliding by the Municipal Corporation (Times of India [Pune edition] 31Oct, 2007), an agreement was reached, and in August 2007, the Solid Waste Collection and Handling (SWaCH) Cooperative was established as the umbrella organization for the waste-pickers involved in doorstep collection. Membership of the Cooperative was open to all, but the KKPKP waste-pickers were given first priority, and after them the next priority for membership were those classified as living in 'below poverty line' (BPL) categories. SWaCH was given responsibility for doorstep collection for 80 of the city's 140 wards and a budget of Rs3.5crore (US$0.7m) to set up and run the programme. The municipal corporation agreed to provide support for five years after which SWaCH was expected to be self-sufficient. The Governing Body of SWaCH comprises 14 waste-pickers/collectors, two representatives of the PMC and one representative of KKPKP. Within a year of its establishment SWaCH was well accepted by the community, and it carefully positioned itself as a proactive service provider offering a range of services to complement doorstep collection. They had their own website advertizing these services (http://swachcoop.com/about-swachpune.html, accessed July 2009): including having drop-off points for householders to leave large items; building compost bins for householders; collecting electronic waste separately; and providing integrated services for institutions like schools, as well as office blocks and corporations. SWaCH looked at providing recycled products such as bags for sanitary pads only to improve the safety of waste-pickers, but it also promoted the recycling message and provided another source of income for the waste-pickers (Times of India [Pune edition] 7 June, 2009). The waste-pickers were also trained in 'soft skills' in customer service and communications, to improve their interaction with their clients: Pune's householders (Times of India [Pune edition] 12 April, 2009).

The KKPKP was also connected to the global waste-picking issues through its advocacy and policy work (Samson 2009). In the 2009 UN Climate Change Convention negotiations, KKPKP spoke out against aspects of the UN's Clean Development Mechanism and argued that the proposal to burn waste for methane production would make thousands of waste-pickers unemployed. The point that KKPKP made was that recycling saved 25 times more greenhouse gases than incineration, and seven times more than landfill. They particularly objected to a Clean Development Fund (CDF) supported 'refuse derived fuel' plant in the Pune landfill, which has reduced the local waste-picker earnings by more than half. "If the waste goes into the incineration plant, what do we eat?" Mr. Gaekwad said' (The Hindu 10 June, 2009). As seen from these case studies KKPKP is driven by the continued struggle for waste-picker rights, as well as raising awareness of the gendered and caste relations inherent in waste-picking.

Gender and waste-pickers

As indicated earlier in this chapter, waste- was highly gendered. It was regarded as such an 'unclean' activity that men of any caste did not want to be engaged in it, and the *dalits* would prefer their womenfolk to be engaged in waste-picking at the household level, while men operated pushcarts from shop to shop picking up recyclable items. The big changes brought about by KKPKP, and especially the SWaCH co-operative, was to essentially change the nature of the work so that it was less stigmatized, more lucrative and involved fewer hours of work. The question that continued to face KKPKP was: how to maintain the access of their members to waste and not be pushed out by male-dominated waste collection processes? The KKPKP was very careful to ensure that it was not a 'women's' union or exclusive in any way, as they felt that while the argument for workers' rights had very strong gender dimensions, to make it exclusive would lead to divisions in the community and enable opponents to adopt divide and rule tactics. The approach that KKPKP took was to ensure the representation in the KKPKP governance represented the proportion of men and women engaged in waste-picking; and that these proportions were maintained as the new systems were implemented to avoid the phenomenon of men 'muscling in' on a sector as technology changes. With technological change it is often the benefits of the technology changes that is accessed by men at the expense of women, and so the challenge for the KKPKP and the SWaCH co-operative was to ensure that did not happen.

The approach taken to protect the women workers here was through strong membership structure through the union. While it was possible for the gender balance in the KKPKP to change over time to include more men, there were two important features that made this unlikely in the short-term: firstly, the requirement that all new members had to cover-off membership subscriptions back to when the union was formed, to limit the level of 'freeloading' that later membership brought; and secondly, the preference given to KKPKP members in doorstop solid waste collection for the city, through the rules that were put in place. The Pune Municipal Corporation could provide contracts to different providers, and as truck collection expanded with more automation this would inevitably occur, but in the short to medium term this was unlikely due to the strength and relative militancy of the KKPKP. In the longer term the children of waste-pickers were not taking up their mothers' occupation, and so in another generation there would be fewer *dalit* women being involved in manual waste-picking. The key change that occurred through KKPKP and SWACH was that the waste-picker women themselves had a strong influence on setting the pace of change.

Conclusion

The waste-picker programme as a development programme is an important case study of success in meeting the broad goals originally envisaged, but also one of institutional sustainability. The programme was initially supported by a relatively small annual grant from an INGO donor over ten years, and in that time the KKPKP was able to build an investment fund from which staff are paid and secretarial costs covered, and to ensure the programme was independent from donor funding. KKPKP has set up a separate co-operative to manage the work of waste-picking itself, so that while the women still operated as individual traders, it was under the umbrella and protection of both a co-operative and a union. From the outset the SNDT sub-centre continued to provide support to the association though mobilization and training programmes with waste-pickers; and it also provided programme management and some secretarial and support type services for the union. Staff from SNDT are effectively seconded to the union and the SWaCH co-operative, to provide the staff resources to these bodies. Some of these staff are the children of waste-pickers. The women reported that they had their dignity restored: rag-picking was, and still is, seen as a dirty and low status occupation, but the KKKP provided it with legitimacy. The women were living in a cleaner environment and had escaped the stigma of being perceived as being dirty, to the point that they '... look[ed] like the rest of the community' when they were not at work (Waste-picker quote 2002). This meant they faced less overt discrimination from the middle class, they could stand up for themselves, and had greater financial literacy with savings and banking. They were able to support their children's education, as they realized there were other options beyond waste-picking for the future generation, and there was also marriage support to prevent child marriage. Finally, they had a greater income with easier and greater access to waste, and they were formally recognized as part of the city's waste management processes.

SNDT had a strong commitment to its values and a strong programme around the pursuit of the rights of the people it served, the waste-pickers. In terms of empowerment, the KKPKP had made a clear difference to the lives of the women, it had given them agency and enabled them to be able to negotiate with police and officials and make decisions around the work of the union. The outcomes of the work of both KKPKP and SWaCH was an effective increase in waste-picker incomes through access to waste, lower costs of credit and more security in their employment. The waste-picker programme adopted a different model to most other NGO programmes, with an emphasis more sharply focused not only of the rights of the women but also their role in the process. They were actively involved in programme priorities identification and design in a formal process through the monthly meetings. There was also a high level of staff accountability to the waste-picking women themselves. Being associated with the University (which largely leaves them alone) the staff were less involved in day to day NGO organizational issues and could focus their energies more directly on the waste-pickers, etc. It was a very successful model in what it set out to do.

5   Measuring women's empowerment

Introduction

The previous chapters looked at the situation of rural NGOs in two districts of Karnataka, and an urban NGO in Pune; and the rapid changes they had to manage in the early 2000s. This chapter will now look at how these and other NGOs are involved in empowerment programmes with self-help groups and the contributing factors in their effectiveness. It will examine, first how empowerment might be measured when it comes to NGO self-help group work, and then the factors that influence empowerment outcomes, especially for the poorer and more marginalized groups. Quantitative and qualitative analyses are both necessary if meaningful insights are to be gained: a qualitative analysis can identify the key factors in, and indicators of empowerment, given its rather nebulous nature and largely cognitive meanings; while a quantitative analysis can provide some indication of the extent of any change and enable comparisons to be made. This mixed method approach is preferable to attempting to identify empirical proxies, which may or may not be valid in a particular context.

The challenge for meaningful research, then, is to be able to score, rank and undertake what is essentially a quantitative analysis of qualitative measures. This way we can ascertain the relative importance of a number of possible factors in achieving empowerment outcomes from NGO interventions. Once these factors are identified, further qualitative analysis is then required to validate these findings and establish if there are causal relationships or merely coincidental associations. The approach taken in this study was to interview around 70 SHGs as focus groups from the set of NGOs being studied, analyse the data, and then follow this up with further interviews of the leadership and staff of the participating NGOs to verify and put some context to the findings. Finally, two workshops were held with the NGOs to discuss the issues raised from the self-help group survey results. The results of the study indicated that 'agency' was the key measure of empowerment, and both the time the group had been functioning and accountability of the NGOs to the self-help groups were key causal factors for empowerment.

Researching empowerment with Indian NGOs

The research involved a survey of 15 NGOs and 77 self-help groups supported by those NGOs. Nine of these NGOs were used as case studies in Chapters 3 and 4. The other five NGOs included: a Christian NGO, Good News, in Dharwad District; an environmental NGO, the Development Academy, in nearby Pune; BGGS, a small rural NGO in Dharwad; YUVA, another urban NGO; and Disha Kendra, an NGO working with tribal communities in Maharashtra. The NGOs were chosen from a list of the NGOs working in the relevant district. Five NGOs were chosen each in Dharwad and Kolar on the basis they represented the range of characteristics and sizes of NGOs working in each District, with the other five NGOs representing NGOs in different settings, namely, urban, environmental and tribal communities by way of comparison. Of course not each NGO was confined to their home district; for example, MYRADA worked across a number of districts in three states, but the NGO work in that district was the focus of the study.

The SHGs that the NGOs were working with were chosen using a stratified random sample so that a range of ages of the groups and the castes of the women with whom the NGOs were working were represented. The principal method used in the research was a group survey, involving the collection of qualitative and quantitative data from the groups. The interaction with the groups also provided the opportunity to capture some of the women's own narratives of how they experienced empowerment. This data was then enumerated and statistically analysed to establish the extent of any change, relevance of the findings, and for comparative purposes. The basis for using the two-stage mixed-method approach in the data analysis was to enable some level of triangulation by using different data sources including statistical rankings, personal narratives and NGO records (Sandelowski 2000). The key concepts being analysed, empowerment and accountability, are both normative, and are not easily subject to empirical testing as they can have different meanings in different cultural settings. It was important then to capture how they were experienced in this part of India. It goes without saying that poor women in India are not a homogenous group, and so no one woman's voice reflects that of all, or even many, marginalized women. Experiences of marginalization and empowerment vary across the regions of India, and so it was important that context specific analyses were undertaken to capture the richness of these experiences in a particular setting (Murthy 2001). There were problems with using a predetermined survey approach in which respondents were 'led' through a series of possible or expected outcomes. These can lead to a range of normative biases where people respond in the way they think the researcher was looking for or expecting. The other issue was that of relationship between the researcher and the subject. The very act of asking the question set up a power relationship between the researcher and the subject that could lead to problems with the quality of the data being collected (Goetz 2001; Reid and Vianna 2001).

The survey used open-ended discussion techniques, allowing more time for free-flowing discussions within the groups as well as with the researcher. The researcher tried to improve access to the groups by sitting with them in an informal manner, and providing background information on the research and other information the groups wanted to know. By using open-ended questions and an analysis of the responses, the indicators for empowerment were developed. As these were described in terms of the broader empowerment literature and 'agency', the links could be readily made (see Chapter 2). For the quantitative analysis of the data the interview responses were categorized into a series of Likert scales. This process involved a number of steps: first, the responses to an open-ended question on changes people had experienced in their lives over time listed and the lists grouped into *taxonomies*, or classifications. The taxonomies were then used to determine a *coherent domain* that positioned items on the list in a way that was more or less consistent across respondents' answers so meaningful comparisons were possible (Hines 1993). The next step was to number and rank the items on the lists to produce a series of interval data as an ordinal rank. The women in the SHGs identified empowerment for them as expanded choice and action, which was the domain; within that the taxonomies were the capacity to: leave the house freely; interact with officials; and participate in local government processes.

These rankings reflected the degree of change the respondents indicated they had experienced. This was further corroborated in the interview, by not only looking at the information per se, but also by examining the interviewees' approach to providing the information, and their level of participation (Poland and Pederson 1998). This approach is similar to a grounded-theory approach, which inductively develops measures, which are then grouped and coded (Webler and Tuler 2000). These findings and associated explanations were then compared with

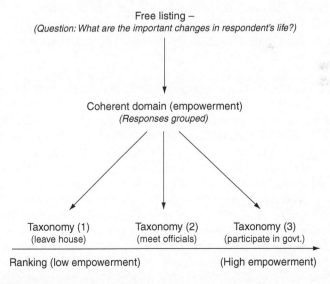

Figure 1 Framework for ranking empowerment.

other similar research, and further qualitative research that occurred with the case study NGOs that looked at how the NGOs themselves define and assess empowerment.

Measuring the variables that affect empowerment

The survey selected the focus groups SHGs from the list the NGO provided of the self-help groups that it was working with. The use of focus groups rather than individual interviews has the advantage of capturing more information in a given time, and it also provides a collective testimony and 'emphasizes empathy and commonality of experience and fosters self-disclosure and self-validation' (Madriz 1998: 116). Typically, the interviews lasted between one and a half and two hours and sought in the first instance factual data on details of the group and its members, and the village. These information questions were then followed up with open-ended questions to elicit information on the changes that had happened to the women through their SHG membership, and how decisions are made both within their household and within the group. The semi-standardized structure allowed for discussion within the groups of the issues as they emerged. There were six broad areas covered in the survey:

- characteristics of the village itself in terms of population, caste, schools and other social amenities such as water supply, formal and informal groups and associations in the village;
- structure of the self-help group in terms of membership, and their endowments such as education and caste;
- decision-making in the SHG;
- the accountability mechanisms the sponsoring NGO has with the groups;
- changes to SHG members in terms of what they had learnt, what they had gained in terms of assets and how their lives had changed;
- village social capital such as decision-making processes and the broader support mechanisms within the village.

Following the survey the ranked numeric data were analysed using non-parametric Spearman tests to calculate the correlation or ρ value of a sample size of 77 groups. This particular test was chosen to avoid assuming a specific distribution for the data. While the sample was relatively small and difficult to randomize due to access difficulties etc., the statistical test gives some indication of the relative importance of certain factors in NGO work on empowerment. Empowerment was the dependent variable in the correlation analysis, with the key independent variables being accountability of the NGO with the groups, and the number of years the group had been meeting together. Other variables based on the endowments of the groups were also tested, but found not to be significant.

The data analysis of the focus group survey data results indicate that both time and accountability were found to be statically correlated with empowerment. A second phase of interviews involving NGO staff and management was then undertaken as a follow-up to look more closely at these two statistically significant factors.

Table 2 Results of Spearman rank correlation

Independent variables	Mean	SD	ρ	p-value
Accountability	2.610	1.1546	0.35	0.0018**
Caste	2.513	1.5894	−0.17	0.1334
Education	1.883	1.3176	0.05	0.6608
Land	2.591	1.3370	−0.13	0.2444
Village social capital	2.948	0.6766	0.06	0.6195
Change in social capital	0.630	0.4700	0.22	0.0589
Size of group	22.234	19.5737	0.04	0.7358
Years of group	3.653	2.4516	0.26	0.0240*

n = 77; Empowerment is the dependent variable
* Significant at the five per cent level
** Significant at the one per cent level

Empowerment

Empowerment was examined through 'agency' by using a set of proxy questions. These questions explored the group members' perceptions of what they had learnt as a result of being active in the group; the key changes in their lives that had occurred during the past few years; and whether the women believed these changes were related to their membership of the SHG. Finally, the questionnaire explored the group members' involvement in broader village life including, inter alia, local government, and how community issues were dealt with. The set of responses to these questions provided data about the change in personal agency the women experienced as a consequence of being a member of a group; as well as what might be called the breadth of empowerment, that is, to the extent that the different members experienced change within a particular group. Other questions relating to empowerment looked at the outcomes the women had experienced, such as what they had learnt and the assets they had gained.

The numeric coding was done by grouping the responses into the five broad categories that emerged from the surveys. These became the *taxonomies* or capabilities that defined empowerment for these women. These were the ability to:

   i go out of the house freely;
  ii meet with officials;
 iii travel independently outside the village;
 iv attend village meetings etc.; and
   v actively participate in local political processes.

A score was then given to the level of empowerment that had been 'experienced' by members of the group with a ranking of 0–5 with 0 being for 'no change' in empowerment and 5 for the highest outcome that could be expected within that context for these groups. The assessment of the data to make the ranking had two components: the content of the responses; and the number of the members of the group who responded. For example, if only a small proportion of group members answered, a lower score was recorded for a particular indicator (such as going out of the house), than if the whole group responded. This method of ranking can be a little problematic in that the social and cultural context of the interview itself may limit the response of some members of the group, given the discussion was held with a foreign man sometimes at relatively short notice, with the discussion on topics that the group did not normally talk about. The responsiveness of the group itself, however, could also be seen as a measure of empowerment in that people with greater agency would be less constrained in different and new social situations. However, the ranking scores and range were based on the responses of the women themselves, and the priority the women gave to a particular factor, and this was then verified from other research and literature. Nevertheless, despite these checks, the ranking could still be argued as normative, based partly on the values and judgements made by the researcher in analysing the testimonies of the respondents. There was also a weakness in using Likert scales for this type of research. There is an inherent assumption that the 'gap' between each numeric factor is constant. That is, the nominal or 'empowerment difference' between a (i) for going out of the house and a (ii) for meeting with officials is the same as the empowerment difference between (ii) meeting with officials and a (iii) going out of the village freely; which of course could not be assumed in that way. But despite these two reservations, this method of data analysis did provide some means to gain an indication of the extent and direction of the changes in empowerment identified by qualitative methods.

The main findings of the study were that first, in terms of empowerment, women themselves identified strongly with notions of 'agency' in how they described the key changes that had occurred in their lives. These changes (albeit often subtle) in power relations with those with whom the women interacted (through their increased agency), were ranked by the women – in terms of importance – ahead of more tangible outcomes, such as increased incomes. The second finding was that there was a strong correlation between empowerment and those NGOs with strong 'downward' accountability mechanisms. These findings supported the notion that empowerment within women's lives, particularly in terms of 'agency', was stronger if the women in the self-help groups had a direct role in some of the institutional processes of the organization that facilitated that change (in this case the NGOs). Most of the responses from the SHGs emphasized a few key indicators of the changes in the lives of their members and provided an insight into how empowerment was perceived and experienced by these groups. These indicators related primarily to improvements in the 'agency' of the women and were categorized broadly as: autonomy of action; changes in family decision-making; participation in community decision-making; and advocacy on broader social issues. These related to the domains of change discussed in Chapter 2, in that the women had greater influence in the family domain, and access to and influence in both the community and political domains.

An interesting and related finding, was that in response to the open-ended question on 'change', only a few respondents mentioned gaining assets or increased

Table 3 Summary of empowerment responses

Key change	Go out of house	Gain family respect	See SHG as important	Attend village meetings	Deal with officials	Social advocacy	Engage in business	Strong influence in community
No. responses (n = 77)	37	21	31	21	28	17	15	13

incomes as such. This suggested that changes in the economic domain, popular with microfinance proponents, do not feature as highly in these women's lives as many would expect. This of course did not mean that increased incomes were not important, but they were not seen as an important change in and of themselves. For these women it was the broader process of social inclusion and their influence in it that they found empowering. A number of respondents, however, did refer to the reduced cost of credit, possibly because it increased the stability of incomes, and the associated increase in certainty in the household economy, was important in their lives. These changes that were reported went beyond the cognitive of how women 'felt'; but they also described how these changes led to tangible effects on their lives. Table 3 summarizes the number of responses to the identified key changes.

Autonomy of action

The capacity for the women to go out of their homes independently of other family members was a clear statement from them of an increased autonomy of action. While *purdah* (the seclusion of women from public) in the strict sense was not followed by any of the members of the SHGs surveyed, the socialization of women in poor Indian households was very strong, and except for agricultural work in season, women were generally restricted in their public movements. There were strong family and social expectations that women would generally stay in the house and undertake household duties. Many of the respondents to the survey referred to the 'four walls' being all they knew. Increased mobility gave women and their SHGs legitimacy in the eyes of other family members, particularly, the husbands who 'allowed' the women to attend the meetings. These groups were seen by the family primarily as savings and credit groups, and so were a means to increase the financial resources available to the household.

The women used phrases such as: 'being able to act independently' to indicate a key change in their lives, which for them was transformative. One group referred to the fact that they 'now had their freedom'; and another group member said she could 'now go to Delhi' (some 2000km away) to emphasize the degree of personal change she had experienced. The implications of the relatively simple act of being able to go out of their home meant that the women could now interact with other members of the community regularly. This included being able to attend SHG meetings on a regular basis and doing the banking work associated with the savings programme. This way they were able to interact with a range of officials, whereas before they joined the SHG, their personal interaction was confined to the family. In the waste-picker community of Pune, the women responded that as a result of the changes the NGO programme had brought to their lives they could now wash twice a day and change their clothes after work, 'and then I look like everybody else'. The implication was that they were being treated the same as others in the community, mainly because they could not be readily identified as 'untouchable' waste-pickers. The increase in self-esteem often resulted in improvements in a number of tangible areas such as the livelihoods for the women and their families, leading to a further increase in the women's personal self-esteem. This supports the theory of 'psychological empowerment' discussed in Chapter 2, where a virtuous circle of heightened self-esteem occurs, leading to tangible results, which in turn boosts self-esteem further.

Dealing with officials and family

The second area of autonomy of action the respondents identified was an increased interaction with local officials: the main ones being bank managers, as the SHGs had to have bank accounts for their savings, and typically, the banking role was rotated among the group members. What was interesting from the data was that in those cases where the banking role was not rotated among the group, the members tended to report fewer [empowering] changes in their lives. While this was not able to be statistically correlated due to a small sample size, it did point to the importance that interacting with new people in new situations and domains can have on people's lives. In most cases the range of officials the women dealt with widened over time: from dealing with bank staff in the first instance, to meeting with government officials about benefits that may be due to group members, and in some cases, village issues that directly affected the group members, such as water supply.

The increased capacity for independent action in many cases led to an increased level of respect from the family and some change in the respondent's power and authority within the household. In one SHG a member referred to having being 'introverted' from harassment, but as a result of the self-help group programme had become 'bold' and gained her 'voice'. It was mainly the husband and his extended family, such as brothers and their in-laws, particularly the mother in-law (who traditionally had some power within Indian families) who had the change in attitudes: phrases like 'I gain more respect in the family'; or 'I am no longer treated like an idiot' were not uncommon responses in the focus groups interviews. A number of women highlighted changes in family decision-making, namely an increased capacity to deal directly with various domestic problems that emerge; for example, small disputes, problems with children, and their education; while others indicated that they could now deal better with household problems that are more serious, such as alcoholism and associated domestic violence by the menfolk.

The importance of education for the children, especially girls, was a common response from most groups. This was driven home to the women when they, as members, had learn to sign their names as part of normal banking transactions, and that provided them with an identity in the broader community. Most SHGs were also required to have an educated person in the group to keep records and undertake other administrative tasks, and those groups that did not have any literate members 'employed' a student, or one of the members' educated children to carry out this task. There were, however, a range of other factors that affected the level of education of girls, of which the intervention of the NGO may be only part of the story. Groups that were very new also reported they were sending their daughters to school, whereas before they would not. Some of the reasons that this was happening were: improved local infrastructure (schools, roads and buses); the spread of television and the 'Hindi' movie and the different portrayals of women these media presented; and the positive role models from other women in the village who were sending their daughters to school. These all contributed to breaking down the traditional practice of keeping the daughters at home. The study found, however, that the SHGs did provide support for girls' education, and so the groups had some role in the increase in the number of girls staying longer at school.

Participation in village political life

The women generally perceived themselves, as a result of their SHG membership, as having *some* influence in village political life, and in some cases the women nominated their participation and influence in village political life as an important change (See Table 2), but this is still in a context where the space for women to participate in village life was limited, with most village processes still being male-dominated and patriarchal. The other main factor influencing the involvement of women in village life was the changes to the system of local government and the introduction of *gram sabhas* (village meetings) as a consultative forum for the *gram panchayat* (village council). Also the affirmative action policy of the Indian government requires that 35 per cent of *gram panchayat* places go to women, and that the District Collector appoints *gram panchayat* chairpersons in such a way as to ensure an adequate representation of women and scheduled castes and scheduled tribes' in these positions. In Dharwad districts where the *gram sabhas* were working well, there was greater participation of women SHG members in these processes. The few women who were elected into the *gram panchayat* indicated that participating in the SHGs provided the support and grounding for them to be able to participate in local government. Thus, membership of SHGs provides an important preparation ground for these broader community processes.

The women also reported a greater role in advocacy on local issues, mainly at the local *gram panchayat* level driven by perceived injustices based on gender and caste biases by officialdom. This advocacy was mainly around improvements to roads, water and village development, and also access to facilities, such as washing facilities by *dalits*. The SHGs were also involved some state government level advocacy, mainly on the issue of having the Government either not issue, or withdraw, licences to sell alcohol in villages. The Government licensed the sale of alcohol for specific villages for which it received a license fee, and as it was an individual licence for a village it was possible to pressure the government to have the licence withdrawn. The main reason that could be argued for a withdrawal of a licence was on the grounds of domestic violence and family safety. As result there was a very active community-based advocacy campaign across the state to have these licenses withdrawn on a case-by-case basis. For the women of these SHGs, being engaged in advocacy represented quite a shift beyond their everyday village life, and more importantly demonstrated the power of them and their SHG in being able to tackle these sensitive issues.

Stability of income

As discussed above, one of the outcomes of the expanded choices and capacity for action the women identified was some improvement in their standard of living. While only a minority of respondents nominated economic benefits in answer to the unprompted open-ended questions on change, the women did recognize the economic benefits that accrued from the intervention in follow-up discussion. This was typically described as having increased assets, ready cash, the reduced cost of credit and general economic stability in the household. These economic outcomes enabled the women to invest in children's education, undertake some income generation and provide household items that they saw as providing a better standard of living. A greater disposable income that reduced cost of credit and provided ready savings led to opportunities for the women to make a broader set of choices. Examples included the upgrading of pottery wheels of a potter caste family, by moving from wood to steel bearings; and in other cases the women purchased small amounts of gold to enable them to obtain secured credit at lower interest rates for themselves (rather than their family) through the commercial banks' pawnbroking services. Other groups reported an increased capacity to send their children to school, the purchase of clothes, and the accumulation of assets such as cattle or goats by many households. For the waste-pickers of Pune, in an urban setting, the chief resource gained was easier access to household waste, their source of livelihood. The economic benefits in both urban and rural areas gave the women a much stronger sense of security not only in economic terms but also in social terms. In the urban areas of Pune, for example, the related social improvement was that the waste-pickers suffered less discrimination following recognition from the municipal authorities, and also to some extent because they could afford better housing and clothing.

The advantages brought by the co-operation and the norms of reciprocity of working together as a SHG, was an important resource for large number of groups. The ability to sit together to discuss issues, solve problems together, 'listen to each other more' and the mutual support for women who were in domestic disputes or being harassed by the police, were all identified as specific benefits. The solidarity within the SHGs was also seen as a source of status; earlier their lives were seen as 'drab' and they were 'treated as idiots', but now the women had status, were getting information and were interacting with people outside their household and the group. From the survey data it is possible to map a progression in empowerment indicators over time in the life of a SHG. In the initial stages of a group's life the women reported access to very basic resources such as the habit of savings, and then access to cheaper credit. The next step involved going out of the house, participating in basic household decisions such as food purchasing and gaining access to paid work outside the house. As confidence and self-awareness grew the group members became involved in SHG management, taking on social issues in the village, etc. and finally taking a greater control in household decision-making. If a personal interest was there, some became involved in the local-level political processes, which was an opportunity for poor women to be involved in local government. Whether a person seeks to become a politician or not is a matter of personal choice rather than an indicator of empowerment. It can be argued, however, that across a district or a number of communities, an increased number of women from marginalized groups being represented in politics may give some indication of broader empowerment processes at play.

Factors that affect empowerment

One of the key findings of the research was the positive correlation of accountability and time (the years SHG had been operating) with empowerment. The scores for accountability were derived from the type of consultative and reporting processes the NGO had to the aid recipients through the SHGs. For the NGOs in this study the range of accountability mechanisms they had in place included: staff listening and responding to the needs of the SHGs; management meeting regularly with these groups (depth of accountability); and more formal mechanisms such as scheduled meetings (level of formality) (Kilby 2006). These latter processes could give high level of control to the recipients, not only of programmes, but even in terms of the strategic direction of the NGO. These accountability processes were given a numeric ranking based on a 0–5 numeric Likert scale. A low ranking (score of 0–2) was given to the more informal and irregular processes the NGO adopted, while a high ranking (score of 4–5) for those processes with a high level of formality and frequency, and an open agenda for the groups to engage with (see Figure 2).

The results showed a strong correlation (a positive ρ value significant at the one per cent level) between the accountability of the NGO to the SHGs and the level of

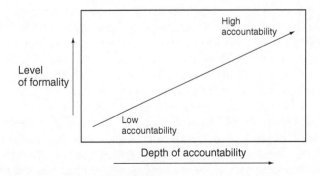

Figure 2 NGO downward accountability.

empowerment of group members. To analyse the accountability mechanisms that these NGOs have towards the SHGs they work with, the NGOs studied were notionally divided into three broad groupings (based on the level of formality of the accountability processes they had in place: *informal* processes; *semi-formal* processes; and *formal* mechanisms for accounting for their work with the groups. These divisions were to some extent arbitrary and were made for the purpose of better describing the accountability processes.

Informal accountability processes

This group of NGOs did not see it as important to have mechanisms to take on the views of the SHGs in terms of how the programme is being delivered, the priorities, and other similar matters. The NGOs saw themselves primarily as service providers or charitable organizations, and therefore the need for formal and semi-formal processes was less important to them than if they were social change agents, where they would be seen to have a more representative role. Women's empowerment, for this group of NGOs, was enabled through the increased opportunities provided by the services or the work that the NGO was providing to these groups and communities, and the increase in the range of choices available to the participants that the programmes provided. The SHGs had the choice of availing themselves of the services or not, if they did not see these services as relevant in their lives. Staff and management of these NGOs felt their interactions were characterized by a sense of solidarity with the groups, and they were mindful of their needs and priorities. While the relationship was informal it was seen as very real, and usually involved a wider group of staff or management engaged with the groups, than only the project staff involved in the project. Overall, this group of NGOs argued that the formal accountability was elsewhere: either to their boards, donors, or government; and their accountability was derived from the provision of specialist services that are widely recognized as being community priorities, and for which there was some need for commonality of approach. Others felt that if they had more formal processes, then expectations would be raised in the community which they would be unable to meet, and so have some difficulties in their programmes and lose the confidence of the community.

For the larger NGOs such as MYRADA, it was important that common approaches were taken across all programmes, and that programme management requirements were such that there would be some certainty in programming, for funding reasons. Informal rather than formal processes were also necessary to avoid expectations being unrealistically raised. The view of MYRADA was that it was the process of empowerment that led to accountability, not the reverse: their argument was that if the recipients were empowered as a consequence of an NGO intervention, then that showed the NGO was accountable to the recipients' needs. The other main feature of this group of agencies is that they did not see themselves as having a primary mediation role between the aid recipients and the government authorities. In all cases there was some brokering between the communities and the government; however, it was largely informal, irregular and non-public. Most of the NGOs in this group saw their institutional priorities as quite separate to their work on the ground, and spent considerable energy dealing with donors and governments. They did not see these institutional processes of expanding into new areas, new communities and new sectors as relevant to their aid recipients. In these cases they felt that direct accountability mechanisms to the groups would in some way compromise them institutionally and limit their capacity for expansion, or dealing with other stakeholders.

Semi-formal accountability processes

Other NGOs in the study readily acknowledged the importance of some level of accountability to their aid recipients, and had put in place a number of what could be described as semi-formal processes for reporting back to the communities with whom they were working. In addition to the practice of management regularly meeting with these communities, these NGOs had processes in place for taking on board the priorities of the aid recipients, and the programming processes of these NGOs were flexible enough to reflect these priorities. However, in these cases the recipients did not directly participate in the organization's business. While representatives from the SHGs attended annual meetings and made suggestions, they did not feel part of the organization in any strict sense of the word. Nevertheless, the management saw some importance in being accountable to the community they were serving and had set up processes to reflect that. In the example of KIDS, the main linkage they had with the community was having the community group leaders visit the KIDS office every month to discuss the programmes. There was a review process every four meetings to discuss what was happening in the groups, and what linkages with government and other organizations the groups wanted. The KIDS' staff asked people what issues were relevant and accepted feedback.

The key to the relationship was that according to KIDS staff 'the community has a certain minimum standard of service' and so KIDS were accountable to the community in meeting their needs. But for KIDS this relationship seemed to go beyond minimum standards: empowerment was seen by KIDS' staff in terms of the women's credibility to go to the banks on their own and have access to the resources of the village. From a staff perspective it was: 'seeing the women free from violence and ill-treatment at a community level and personal level [that] was the strongest form of accountability' (Interview KIDS 2002). To some extent this reflected the same point that MYRADA had made to justify its informal approach, but in the case of KIDS there were additional processes in place. The NGOs in this group that had semi-formal processes saw their role in broader terms than service provision (leading to empowerment) but rather more as a catalyst for local level social action. In the case of KIDS this catalytic role was in respect of the rights of children and women, especially the more marginalized groups such as sex-workers and street kids. In the case of Chinyard the catalytic role was concerned with village-based social problems such as alcoholism, dowry or other 'social ills' brought to them by the groups they were working with. These NGOs responded by forming a loose partnership with these groups, and the NGOs took a brokering, rather than a representative role, in dealing with social issues. It was the groups themselves who dealt with the issues, with the help of the NGOs, rather than the NGOs undertaking this role themselves. It was these semi-formal processes of accountability that the NGOs used to ensure their work and interventions were relevant.

Formal accountability processes

This group of NGOs relied on strong personal associations and formal feedback mechanisms to offer the SHGs and communities they were working with the opportunity to put their views for the management of the NGOs to consider in their programming. These mechanisms varied considerably among the NGOs surveyed, but reflected the approaches the organizations had taken to overcoming the dilemma of being an organization with a public benefit purpose (rather than a mutual benefit organization like a co-operative), while at the same time being able to be held to account by their aid recipients. For example, the process adopted by IDS encouraged their board members to make contact with the groups directly so the board was directly in touch with those it saw as its constituents. Each board member met with a number of groups in a particular village, or group of villages, prior to board meetings. In this way board members performed a representative function by putting the aid recipients' point of view at the highest level, even though they were not elected by them. This approach reflected the de facto role a local NGO Board had, and that was to ensure programme effectiveness and that the interests of the aid recipients were being met.

The urban NGO, SNDT, in its work with waste-pickers on the other hand, had regular and direct staff dialogue with an open forum of the group it worked with, the waste-pickers' union – KKPKP. This took the form of a monthly meeting between the small number of staff of SNDT and two representatives of the waste-picker women from each of the 100 slums in which SNDT was working. In practice not all attended, but around 50 women usually went to these meetings, and the discussion was very robust and open, with very controversial issues discussed and difficult decisions hammered out. For SNDT these processes were adopted by the organization because they felt that if empowerment was to occur, the women themselves should exercise a large degree of control, not only over the programme but also, and more controversially, over the NGO staff directly. In this way they would be able to claim some ownership over both the NGO and the programme. In effect SNDT was a contractor to the waste-picker women and their union, and to some extent taking direction from them. In the case of the backdating fees for new members (see Chapter 4), there was a difference in view between SNDT staff and the union, and the union prevailed. The issue that SNDT was non-compromizing on was its opposition to both child labour and communalism (where communities are in conflict with each other on the basis of caste or religion). These issues, in waste-picker communities could be both serious and divisive, as well as being against the law and a denial of rights.

Each of these NGOs, to some extent, fostered the development of a self-managed people's organization, as a representative body to which the NGO provides specific services and expertise. These self-managed organizations are very common in southern India; however, not all have a direct representative function to the NGO, with most solely involved in a co-ordination of microfinance activities among the groups. There they acted as a broker and managed autonomous microfinance practices rather than giving direction to the NGO. In the cases where there was a direct relationship with the NGOs such as in the case of Gram Vikas and IDS, the federations were seen as the path to sustainability of the programme with the plan being that the groups would take over the programme over time. Federation structures can themselves have accountability problems to their own constituencies, with an ongoing relationship, if not dependency, on the NGO. For those federations with Grama Vikas and IDS, there was some NGO staff involvement in their oversight even after some time.

For SNDT and Grama Vikas the relevant representative organizations were not only instrumental in the management of the programme activities, but also influenced the strategic direction of the programme, and even the NGO itself. Grama Vikas was instrumental in establishing the Grameena Mahila Okkuta (the local women's federation) in 1997, which was responsible for not only microfinance activities, but also for strategic issues such as networking with other like-minded organizations and influencing government policy. The role of Grama Vikas in this case was to support the work of the Okkuta rather than taking on an instrumental role itself. In the case of SNDT, the union (KKPKP) took all decisions of a strategic nature that affected it, and the union had a more direct role in setting the work programme and strategic direction of the SNDT. For Grama Vikas, as an NGO it was only involved in new programmes, dealing with donors, and macro-level advocacy. The Grameena Mahila Okkuta was involved in the ongoing programme management, local level advocacy, shared control of the accounts and (increasingly) some donor liaison. In addition, Grama Vikas staff were specifically trained and encouraged to be supportive and responsive to the women's groups. The role of Grama Vikas was becoming more that of a supporting organization and the provider of a venue and logistical support, rather than of an intermediary as such.

These three broad categories of accountability of NGOs as non-representative bodies to the aid recipients were important, as they showed the various mechanisms of accountability that NGOs could have without themselves being membership organizations. It is worth noting, though, that while there were clear processes of accountability, the only real sanction in place for the aid recipients was to pull out of the relationship; there were no real intermediate options for them beyond moral suasion. This analysis of the different types of relationship of NGOs with the groups they are working with can be linked back to the analysis of the empowerment data that show a positive correlation with the accountability mechanisms and empowerment outcomes. The finding of the follow-up study with the participating NGOs was that there were possible accountability options, short of formal membership structures, in which NGOs could account for their work to the aid recipients, and that these are important for strong empowerment outcomes for those groups.

The age of the group

The second factor that showed a positive correlation with empowerment was the age of the group in terms of the number of years it had been functioning, which of itself is not unexpected. An implication of this finding was that a balance should be struck between efficiency, the time spent with a group, and effectiveness, the empowerment outcomes that more time with a group may bring (Berg et al. 1998; Hishigsuren 2000). The NGOs surveyed indicate that many donors, and particularly Government ones, seek to limit the period of the NGO engagement with the SHGs. Many microfinance and other group-support program donors seek a relatively early withdrawal by the NGO from providing support for the groups, usually within three to five years. MYRADA's policy, for example, called for the withdrawal of its staff animators within three years after group formation, seemingly regardless of the endowments or capabilities of group members (Fernandez 1998). While this approach made sense in terms of freeing-up resources for NGO expansion into new villages and communities, it ran the risk of jeopardizing the sustainability of the groups and the empowerment outcomes. There is also the danger of prescriptive policy approaches, so that staff targeted those in the communities who are more likely to be able to 'go it alone' after three years rather than the most needy.

As the findings suggest, these time limits affected the possible empowerment outcomes, particularly for the most poor and marginalized groups such as *dalits*. Here the level of disempowering socialization was such that three to five years was nowhere near enough time, and the case studies indicated that double this period to 10 or more years was necessary in most cases with marginalized groups. While the waste-picker programme was undoubtedly a phenomenal success, the engagement with SNDT and the staff with them was over 15 years. The period of engagement by NGOs with a particular community group was one in which the managerial, and often donor-led, search for efficiency and relatively quick results can led to poor outcomes.

Empowerment in practice

These research findings support the ideas of empowerment that come from sociology and psychology: that is that increased personal agency and self-esteem are the core changes in people's lives that then can lead to social change. Personal changes in self-esteem and agency led to the greater engagement of women in the broader social and economic spheres in their communities, which is in line with other research looking at empowerment from different perspectives and in different country contexts [for example, see (Kabeer 1999)]. It is from enhanced agency that access to resources and tangible outcomes in people's lives follow. While Kabeer argues that agency alone is not sufficient, the women in this research described the empowering processes in their day-to-day lives in terms of changes in their personal agency: the majority of the women surveyed referred quite specifically to an increase in their personal capacity to engage with others, as the most important change they had experienced. In practice, this occurs in a number of different domains: within their families; with others in positions of power outside the household such as bank managers; and also within the self-help group itself. These changes did not mean that women were not susceptible to subsequent shifts in their social environment that were disempowering. For example, in Pune, when the Municipal Corporation's moved a waste dump, from which waste-pickers derived their living, they felt disempowered and helpless. But overall the key change was the increased range of choices and opportunities for action available to the women. A modification to Kabeer's framework might be that resources and tangible outcomes were not only a result of agency, but they also served as a foundation to maintain any changes in personal agency that occurred.

The change in an individual's agency was important as it facilitated the development of relationships outside the immediate household sphere: the women responded to the question about changes in their lives by speaking of being able to go out and gain access to, and influence other relationships that exist in domains outside the household. These were broadly the economic, social and political domains that are found within a village community, and power is related to access to these different domains (Giddens 1979). The change in the respondents' agency expanded the choices available to women personally, and increased the number and range of relationships available to them in different social and political domains. It was these relationships which were a source of power (Narayan 1999; Sen, A. 1999; Vijayalakshmi 2001); and the converse was also true, that it is the denial of access to these domains and relationships which was disempowering. Poverty, when seen as deprivation and marginalization, had a clear political dimension, and was intrinsically related to power relations and the restricted access to different domains within a community (Goetz and Gupta 1996; Kabeer 2001; Zaman 1999). It was the existing conditions of social exclusion and disempowerment that drove how these responses were articulated.

Women's perceptions of empowerment

The approach taken to the research was to examine the phenomenon of empowerment from the marginalized women respondents' perspective. Their narratives of the personal changes they had experienced since the NGO had been working with them were sought. The results, as outlined above, found that the women saw the improvement in their agency as the change that most readily came to their mind, leading to increased self-esteem and self-respect, which they readily contrasted to their social exclusion and disempowerment. The responses of the members of the majority of SHGs to the changes that these NGO savings and credit programmes brought, was a sense that there were greater choices available in their social lives that an effective increase in their disposable income gave them. This change was not seen as increased or stable incomes per se, but rather increased self-esteem and the reduced stress – probably due to the relatively personal nature of the contact with money lenders, which can be personally threatening, not to mention the higher cost of money.

The 'empowerment' that the women have described above had both individual and collective dimensions. At an individual level the women saw the changes they experienced very personally in terms of their agency, and expressed it in terms of an increase in the range of activities they could engage in. These changes were from the very basic one of being able 'to go out of the house now', through to the Pune waste-pickers engaging in political negotiations with respect to their work conditions, and taking control of aspects of city waste collection. These changes, importantly, were directly related to the women's participation within the groups, supporting the idea that power has a collective dimension (Giddens 1979). It was the women's own capacities to make the SHGs more effective that had a strong personal effect on the women. There was a feedback loop operating within the groups with the individual woman's engagement with the groups making the groups more effective, which in turn increased the feeling of self-worth of the individual that then fed back into the group (Drury and Reicher 1999). This collective process had implications for how the groups were established and the norms under which they operated, in particular the relationship the NGO facilitating the group had with the members, and the participation processes in the SHGs that the NGO promoted.

These findings support the argument that empowerment is primarily a social and psychological phenomenon, and is related to access to social resources and power, involving complex interrelationships between the personal and collective domains of women's lives. When asked about the important changes they had experienced in their lives, the women tended to relate the changes they had experienced in personal agency to the work of the SHG. The field of community psychology tends to looks at empowerment in terms of self-knowledge and self-esteem, reduced feelings of alienation and enhanced feelings of solidarity and legitimacy, all of which are related to group interactions (Asthana 1996). These findings also support the feminist view of empowerment, which goes beyond the psychological, to support a broader socio-political view of power relations (Goetz 2001; Jandhyala 1998; Puroshothaman 1998). That is, the increased agency leads to women feeling much better about themselves – greater self-esteem; and they also experience changes in their power, so they are able to influence others and their actions. The most serious deprivation that marginalized people experience (in the context of rural India) is in the social and political sphere rather than the economic. This can have implications for those programmes that focus on 'economic empowerment' and argue that it is a source from which social and political empowerment emerges (Hashemi et al. 1996; Hishigsuren 2000; Schneider 1999). This study supports an alternative view, that is, 'economic generation must be accompanied by social regeneration' (Campbell and Jovchelovitch 2000: 263); and suggests that economic programmes can at best be a means to an end, and must be accompanied by social programmes, with a big say in them coming from the aid recipients themselves.

Empowerment in the household

Analysing the nature of empowerment and disempowerment at the household level is generally more difficult than at the broader community or individual level, mainly because of the normative nature of both the question and the answer in any survey. The values of the inquirer are implicit in any questioning of household relationships; with an implicit value that equality in decision-making is preferable to a situation of one party (overwhelmingly the man) in a relationship assuming the decision-making role. In our own lives we are often happy to delegate a whole range of decision-making to others. Looking at changes in decision-making, however, is valid as power relations invariably involve the locus of decision-making. The second difficulty with looking at empowerment at the household level is more problematic, and that is people often will answer normatively, that is, in terms of 'what should be' rather than 'what is'. The changes the women from the SHGs reported during the focus group discussions usually only obliquely referred to their situation before they joined the self-help groups, such as being unable to go out of the house, or having to seek permission from the husband for any action they wished to take. There was little direct discussion in the focus groups of the power relations in the household, but when there was any such discussion, I would argue that this in itself is an indicator of empowerment, as a level of self-knowledge and analysis is implicit in any such discussion.

The main reason given by the women for any change (albeit often slight) in the power relations in the household, was due to their participation in the SHG, and the consequent change in their role in the household economy. Because the women could access the NGO programmes through these groups, it gave them some legitimacy within the household as these programmes usually brought additional resources to the household. Often this led to a greater level of inclusion of the woman in household decision-making processes with many respondents reporting that they were consulted about household decisions. At a policy level if these often small changes at the household power relations were important in the women's perceptions of the outcomes of the programmes, then a more direct focus by NGOs on these self-identified empowerment outcomes at household level would lead to more effective programmes.

Social exclusion

While the study did not look specifically at how women saw their situation in terms of marginalization or exclusion as a result of their caste or other dependent relationships, the data did provide an indirect view of how poor women saw themselves in their communities and their families. These women not only experienced a heavily restricted household life, but there was also social exclusion from the political and economic spheres of their communities. The extent of this exclusion depended on their caste and class; with 'caste' being a function of their birthright, and 'class' in the Indian context being related to wealth and income. For example, there were cases where tribal women were specifically excluded from the political and broader economic sphere, even following involvement in the SHGs; and for *dalit* women the exclusion from certain spheres extended to relatively mundane areas, such as access to water. The nature of this exclusion was heavily socialized so there was no need for overt enforcement processes. The dalit women *believed* they were being excluded, by virtue of the 'untouchable' nature of their caste. For example, they did not have an entitlement or right to the water from the village well as it would be 'unclean for higher castes', so they did not use it. In an example reported in the survey, when as a result of being in a SHG and the NGO work with it, some women eventually did use the well with no repercussions, they described this relatively simple process as being transformatory: it heightened their self-esteem and confidence. The change in all of these cases was in terms of women's agency – the capacity to have expanded choices – and to be able to take decisions that influence the lives of others. In this case it effected change in what were deeply socialized relationships across caste lines.

The causal factors in empowerment

The factors that show a significant positive correlation with empowerment are important to consider in the NGO discourse on empowerment. The findings on accountability and time can give direction to how NGO empowerment programmes may be implemented; and secondly, they give some direction for future research on empowerment programmes. The accountability of an NGO to the groups with which it was working was a significant factor in achieving strong empowerment outcomes, and supports the view that the exercise of power is in part the ability to call people to account, and power is exercised when one party holds another party accountable for their actions (Day and Klein 1987) – the process of holding another to account is an empowering one. Other research, while not looking at empowerment as such, found that greater levels of participation in decision-making processes led to improved social outcomes, largely due to shifts in authority and control (Blair 2000; Lee et al. 1999; Smith-Sreen 1995). These findings add to this existing research by showing that greater levels of 'downward' accountability were also associated with the empowerment of the poor and marginalized in developing countries. That is, the accountability processes an NGO employs in its relations with its constituents can lead to positive changes in power relations that disempowered individuals experience in their day-to-day lives.

Generally poor and marginalized women in India had no say in calling to account other people, either within their family or outside; they were generally excluded from decision-making at both household and village level, and had few opportunities to engage with other people, let alone be able to hold people to account for their actions (Janardhan 1995). In this context being able to hold NGOs and their staff to account for their work with poor women was unique in their lives, and by its nature was empowering. This empowering change extended beyond the group's relationships with the NGO, to other political, social and economic domains in the women's lives. Key to this is that it was also the level of formality or certainty in the accountability processes that was important in empowerment, and it was this level of formality that established a *right* to participate in decision-making (Joshi and Moore 2000). It was more difficult, or rather there was less incentive, for the NGOs to have formal processes in place for their accountability to the people with whom they were working, because as public benefit organizations they did not have statutory or formal mechanisms for accountability to the aid recipients. This study has found, however, that this structural issue need not be an impediment, as some NGOs had established quite clear mechanisms to transfer some control to the people with whom they were working. The role in the accountability of the NGO through its staff to the community it is working with, was also important for another reason: the staff of NGOs were generally outsiders (in terms of class, caste and origin), in relation to the aid recipients. The ability to hold outsiders (with a perceived higher status) to account was a powerful symbol for marginalized women, and exposed them to new domains of power. What these case studies have shown is that one of the few arenas in which village women can be involved in decision-making processes or exercising agency in a different domain was with the NGO; that is, if it had processes in place for this to happen.

These findings on accountability point to the desirability of NGOs having direct mechanisms of accountability to the communities they are working with if empowerment is to be maximized; but they also showed a fundamental limitation of NGOs as empowerment agents. If NGOs are not required to be accountable they are less likely to hand over power to their constituency: '[one is] sceptical of the capacity or willingness of any but the most exceptional organizations to encourage or even tolerate the autonomous and potentially antagonistic mobilization of their own client groups' (Joshi and Moore 2000: 49).

There is a tension between the source of authority and power within an NGO, and the desire for effective empowerment programmes. All of the NGOs that participated in the research recognized, to varying degrees, the importance of some level of accountability to the recipients if they were to be effective. This was not only for transparency reasons but most also recognized, that this form of accountability was part of good development practice. However, of the 15 NGOs surveyed only one handed power over in a direct sense (SNDT), and two others actively promoted a direct role of their constituency in strategic programming; indicating that any handing over of control to the aid recipients is both difficult and unusual.

NGOs' perceptions of empowerment

Few of the NGOs surveyed saw their accountability to their constituency as an empowering process in itself. SNDT, and Grama Vikas to a lesser extent, were the exceptions; they both recognized that being involved with *dalits*, and having the NGO staff directly accountable to the *dalit* communities, was seen as a way of breaking down caste consciousness. As *dalits* were generally regarded as social outcastes, the members of the broader community were unlikely to see themselves as having any accountability obligations to them. How the staff of SNDT related to the waste-pickers was important in how the waste-pickers would respond. In the waste-pickers' day-to-day dealings with others in the community, such as merchants, more feudal norms of behaviour emerged, and so SNDT saw it as central to their work, and the empowerment of the women, that their approach to the waste-pickers was as 'insiders' together, which should lead over time to some change in the women's own self-perception and self confidence. Likewise the *dalits*, after working with Grama Vikas, also had a high level of confidence in their dealings with higher caste people.

Dalit people power

In Kolar during a government sponsored food-for-work programme for the most drought affected, which involved manually de–silting tanks, some women who Grama Vikas had been working with had to hire tractors from the higher caste people (from the *reddy* caste) in the villages. Initially the tractor owners refused to deal with the women directly (wishing to maintain untouchability), but rather through intermediaries. The women themselves insisted on dealing with the tractor owners directly and 'held out' for three weeks before the tractor owners agreed to deal with the women directly. It was the close interaction with staff at all levels, which gave the women the confidence to deal with higher caste village people in this way.

Apart from these two exceptions, the findings from the research was that the NGOs' own perceptions of empowerment as a goal of their intervention, differed in some key respects from the women's own perceptions of empowerment. The NGOs tended to see the results of empowerment work in tangible terms, such as income or participation in the credit schemes. This view was supported not only in the testimony of the NGO staff, but also in how their programmes were monitored and reported by the NGOs themselves. This was also related to the nature of project interventions and donor expectations which sought tangible outcomes in a relatively confined time period. While the majority of the NGOs in the study saw empowerment as an outcome of their particular intervention, from their point of view empowerment was seen as an overarching goal that would follow a particular intervention – empowerment should be the product of increased incomes, access to credit etc., rather than a direct outcome of the group processes facilitated by the NGOs. This position tends to support the economic paradigm of empowerment outlined by Schneider (1999) and others. Some NGOs in the study focused exclusively on self-help groups as microfinance agents, with their day-to-day interventions and monitoring mechanisms focused exclusively on ensuring the financial aspects of the programme were being maintained. While Chinyard had as its primary objective empowerment so that women 'can participate in local level political processes' (Abbi 1999: 8), neither Abbi's review nor Chinyard's other documents systematically recorded this process in terms of its outreach, but rather saw empowerment as a bi-product of the savings and credit programmes. MYRADA also has clear empowerment objectives, but again tended to see empowerment as a result of their interventions, rather than a specific part of an intervention (Fernandez 2001). The NGOs which did have specific support mechanisms for empowerment such as IDS, BGSS, Grama Vikas and the Development Academy, all found it difficult to monitor empowerment, and depended on anecdotal evidence of specific cases rather than broad-based survey work. At a practical day-to-day level the term empowerment is not looked at, but rather these NGOs would see participatory and governance processes within groups, as well as encouraging groups to deal with their own social priorities, as their way of directly addressing empowerment issues. The strong move to promoting microfinance and financial sustainability in microfinance by NGO funders, particularly by Indian government agencies, was an issue that could have negative effect on empowerment outcomes. This funding regime effectively privileged what can be referred to as instrumental concerns (programme efficiency through financial performance) over social effectiveness. These case studies did not support the view that a well-functioning microfinance programme will automatically result in strong empowerment outcomes (Hashemi et al. 1996). The NGOs that tended to have the highest empowerment ranking were those that had a broader socio-political approach to their development work; that is, SNDT, Gram Vikas and IDS.

New approaches to empowerment evaluation

The approach of the research in eliciting the women's narrative is very important as it has given a perspective on empowerment outside the NGOs' (and the researcher's) expectations and values, and it also provided a common base for making comparisons. It may well be that NGOs would be better served if they looked at the outcomes of their programmes in terms of empowerment, less by way of anecdotal evidence, which may reflect a minority of cases, but more by way of systematic monitoring of the broad-based changes women see in their lives. This may require the development of specific instruments for the NGOs to use. The current instruments such as PIMS used by MYRADA, and AIMS developed by Management Systems International for the World Bank in microfinance, tended to focus on pre-existing outcomes, which could skew the results, rather than on open-ended approaches that enabled the views of the beneficiaries of a programme to be heard more directly. The lesson that emerged from the difference in the women's views of what is empowering and the NGOs' expectations, is that it pointed to some changes in approaches to group mobilization and management within NGO programmes. If this learning could be developed into practical approaches, NGO work would be more responsive to the self-defined aspirations of the communities with which they were working.

Conclusion

Two key points have emerged from the results of the study: first is that members of the self-help groups identify quite strongly with agency in describing the key changes in their lives following an NGO intervention, even though this may not have been the main objective of the intervention. The change in agency was in terms of the women's capacity to enter different spheres in a community's social, economic and political life. Before the intervention the women were restricted to the household sphere, and there they had little power. Empowerment for these women was being able to enter new spheres or domains and exercise some power over other people's behaviour. The result of this enhanced access to different domains of power was articulated principally in terms of personal self-esteem, expanded choices and the capacity to act. The women in the groups related this change to their interaction with self-help groups they were part of. A feedback loop occurred in that as the self-confidence of the members fed into the group effectiveness, it then fed back into personal agency. This finding is in line with theories of community psychology (Drury and Reicher 1999). It is important because it moved away from the idea of the group being an instrument in providing financial or other 'practical' support to the individual, to the group being an integral part of the process of individual empowerment, and intrinsically tied up with the individual's notion of empowerment.

Second is that the key factors that affected empowerment were the age of the groups and the accountability of the NGO to the groups. While the findings on the age of the group were to some extent expected, the findings on accountability were important as they provided direction for future programming options. Accountability to the aid recipients was important, because when the staff and management of an NGO were being held to account by the group members, this act of accountability was an empowering process, and the group members felt they had some power over the NGO. If poor and marginalized women had power over an external agent such as an NGO (which represented a completely new sphere of influence) then they felt they could expand this influence or power to other spheres in their lives. More broadly, if poverty is seen to some extent as social, economic and political marginalization, which Sen, G. (1999), Narayan (1999) and others argue, then these empowerment processes are important in development practice. Neither of these two factors – time and accountability – which were found to be correlated with empowerment, are dealt with in any detail in the NGO discourse on community development, group formation, or group management. This omission in the NGO discourse and learning practice, may go some way to explaining why strong empowerment results are not common across NGO programmes.

6   NGO accountability

Introduction

As discussed in the previous chapter, the 'downward' accountability of NGOs to the people they are working with is a factor in contributing towards strong empowerment outcomes for poor women in India. This has the obvious implication that strengthening NGO accountability mechanisms to the aid recipients will lead to better empowerment outcomes in NGO practice. NGOs, however, generally do not directly address the issue of 'downward' accountability, as they see themselves having other sets of accountability requirements which have greater priority. This chapter will look at the reasons behind this. It can be argued that NGOs' values are their primary point of accountability, rather than the people they are working with. As we have seen from Chapter 1, NGOs are primarily values-based public benefit organizations (Kilby 2006; Lissner 1977; Tandon 1995a); however, this is rarely examined by donors or in the contemporary NGO discourse. The exceptions to this are the more radical political NGOs, or those NGOs providing sexual and reproductive health and other contentious social policies, both of which have had their government donor funding cut from time to time. For many NGOs, their values play a central role in their management choices, and the development approaches they take. While I argue in this chapter that it is mainly the NGO's values which will decide the approach as to how it should be accountable to its aid recipients, there is also a complex interplay of relations between NGOs, the communities they work with, the government, and donors. These influence how an NGO can realize its values and empower communities, and I would argue that over time it seems that the accountability pressures from this interplay with government and donors can create a shift in the values of the NGO, which has implications for their work, and how they are accountable to their aid recipients.

Most of the NGOs that are included in this study devoted considerable resources to being accountable to their donors. How they managed this was very important to them, as it affected their operations. The shift from being largely reliant on international donors in the late 1990s to being reliant on domestic donors by 2009 showed how important this relationship was to these NGOs, and how it affected each of them differently. While many of these NGOs were not dependent on a single donor, and some of the NGOs such as SNDT had in fact initiated the ending of their funding relationship with INGOs, the source of funding was important, and a driving force for most of these NGOs in terms of their accountability relationships. Accountability to government as a regulator, however, was less important for these NGOs, who saw the reports they have to provide as a requirement or obligation, rather than as part of an ongoing relationship they feel part of. As one NGO manager put it 'we are accountable to the government but we don't feel accountable to the government'. While most NGOs were required to have some level of relationship with the state and federal government, this was not required at the *gram panchayat* level. This is where one would expect NGO to have a close relationship, but few of the NGOs surveyed saw that they needed to have a specific relationship with the *gram panchayat*, and to some extent they were in competition with them in their work with local communities. These accountability relationships that NGOs have with donors and governments have policy implications for NGO programming to meet the empowerment objectives they espouse. There are also implications for how INGO donors see the work they are supporting, and the key features of effective programming around empowerment. The next section will look at these issues in more detail, what the literature and theory says about NGO accountability, and then the extent to which the case studies accord with it.

Accountability

A useful definition of accountability for NGOs, as a starting point for this discussion, is that it is about the conduct and performance of an organization (Day and Klein 1987). However, this is not a simple matter of reports and accounts, rather it is as much about perception and power (Conger and Kanungo 1988; Gray et al. 1997). Accountability generally:

- identifies shared expectations;
- provides a common currency for justification;
- puts agreements into context;
- provides a sense of obligation; or a right to be called to account; and
- has sanctions for failures to meet expectations.

Accountability also defines the relationship between actors through what Schedler (1999) calls 'answerability'; of who can call whom to account, and who owes a duty of explanation. This then establishes a power relationship, with the roles, forms and direction of accountability defining the distribution of authority: '... the notion of authority as the right to call people to account needs to be complemented by the notion of power as the ability to call people to account ... effective power whether legitimate or not in turn requires effective control for accountability' (Day and Klein 1987: 9). While being unable to hold others to account is synonymous with a lack of power, to be unaccountable to others is to be all-powerful, and also be able to provide an illusion of accountability under the guise of responsibility:

> While accountability builds on the modern idea that power and knowledge are separate goods, the notion of responsibility allows powerful actors to maintain

the illusion that they know what they are doing and therefore to dismiss irritating questions that do nothing but disturb their solemn and responsible exercise of power

(Schedler 1999: 19)

Being accountable, therefore, is more than providing access to information but goes a step further and enables the receiver of the information to be able to do something about it, through processes that in the end have sanctions associated with them (Mulgan 2001). This ability to hold agencies to account is an area in which the very poor often lack capacity (Jenkins and Goetz 1999). Because this point is supported by the data presented in Chapter 5, it is easy to argue that the nature of the accountability of an NGO to its aid recipients is central to the empowerment process, as it determines the distribution of power between the NGO and the communities it is working with. However, due to failures in accountability, this occurs a lot less than expected.

NGOs and accountability

While the previous section highlighted the range of accountabilities NGOs might face, it is NGOs' perceived lack of accountability, particularly to those they are working with, that needs to be teased out. Goetz (2006) argues that the failure of NGOs to be accountable to their aid recipients falls into four broad areas:

- Substance: here the NGO in self-help group programmes fails to see that the violations of women's rights or the neglect of their needs in the programmes are accountability failures, or even problems – here the NGO fails to understand or accept that they have an obligation.
- Seekers: the SHGs as seekers lack the leverage to demand answers from power-holders (in this case the NGO). The women are not seen as individual rights bearers, and do not see themselves as such. The cultural context they are embedded in does not give them this privilege.
- Targets: Who is accountable? NGOs? Donors? Governments? Here the multi-level governance structures of many development programmes confuse the lines of accountability.
- Methods: Key accountability institutions are inaccessible to poor women. Can women really take an NGO to court, especially in a collective action or public interest case?

For the reasons above, the question to ask is: how do NGOs manage accountability, and how can the aid recipient hold them to account.

Organizational accountability is empowering when organizations are opened up to their members (Conger and Kanungo 1988; Murthy 2001; Peters and Pierre 2000) and empowerment is related to 'inclusiveness, transparency, accountability and ... legitimacy [through] collective decision-making, collective action and popular participation' (Titi and Singh 1995: 13). As we have already seen in this chapter, the accountabilities that NGOs have to respond to are complex and diffuse, and the tools of enforcement are limited (Ferejohn 1999). There are three broad account-abilities that NGOs have to meet: to their values and mission; to their performance in relation to the mission; and a functional accountability, which is to do with probity (Tandon 1995a). This set of accountabilities is generally to the recipients, donors, the state (Edwards and Hulme 1995) and their values (Edwards 1999a; Edwards 1999b; McDonald 1999). The problem that NGOs have is how to privilege accountability to the aid recipients in this complex accountability environment.

In Chapter 5, it was found that empowerment is correlated with NGO account-ability to the recipients of the aid programme, so it can be argued that the accountability to donors and the state (through the required practice or regulation) can play a part in either supporting or undermining this accountability. It can also be argued that strong 'downward' accountability pressures can hinder NGO expansion and other strategic initiatives, as the people with whom they are working like to keep the NGO programmes to themselves rather than promote an expansion to a broader constituency (Desai and Howes 1995), but this is rarely found to be an issue given the power relations at play in NGO programmes. The question this chapter is concerned with is whether, at a local level, an NGO can be effective in empower-ment if it does not have internal mechanisms of accountability to its aid recipients. If empowerment is the objective then evidence from Chapter 5 and elsewhere would suggest that the accountability structure *has* to be towards the community the NGO is working with, and the social change objectives have to remain foremost (Smith-Sreen 1995). This could even be within the context of humanitarian relief programmes where such structures are harder to establish (Slim 1997). The ques-tion then is: how should an NGO prioritize accountability to the constituency, when there is no simple model and there are competing accountability forces which it faces? As Fox and Brown (1998: 21) note 'although they usually lack formal institutional accountability mechanisms their [NGOs] dependence on maintaining at least the appearance of consistency between theory and practice creates informal, inconsistent, but often powerful accountability pressures'. There is not a single rule for account-ability of NGOs; however, there are some guides in the form of codes of conduct and donor contracts that usually prescribe the accountability processes in the direction of either the private or public donor, or the government as regulator. It is rare, however, that there are requirements for accountability to the aid recipients. This struggle within NGOs reflects the natural tension of: adherence to values; the desire to survive and expand; avoiding 'biting the hand that feeds' (often the state); and maximizing income (Edwards 1997; Lissner 1977). What emerges is that the ideal of accountability of NGOs to their aid recipients is continually under pressure from donors, the state, and the organization's own leadership structures and values. There are also internal accountabilities of staff to each other and management, and from time to time accountabilities to other organizations in networks or where joint programmes are underway, but for this discussion I will focus on the principal (mainly external) accountabilities they face. From the discussion above, a framework of NGO accountability can be developed (Figure 3) which shows four accountabilities that an NGO manages: to its values, recipients, donors, and government.

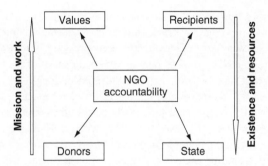

Figure 3   NGO accountabilities.

The top half of the figure (especially when referring to empowerment NGOs) concerns the mission of the NGO and its work, while the bottom half is more instrumental, concerned with their continued existence, and the flow of resources to the NGO. There is a natural tension between the 'top half' – values and constituency – and the 'bottom half' – resources and regulation. This chapter argues that how NGOs manage this tension affects the effectiveness of their work on empowerment.

Accountability to the state and donors

The accountability of NGOs is constantly tested by the state: Firstly, the state is a source of NGO legitimacy through formal legal sanction and registration processes. Second, the state is often a donor through its provision of resources either as direct grants or tax concessions, an increasing issue for Indian NGOs as we have seen in Chapter 3. The effect of these pressures from the state is to move the focus of accountability back to itself. From the state's point of view, social mobilization is at best a lesser priority, and in the case of India it can be seen as a threat. Therefore, NGO performance is increasingly measured according to the managerial and market values of efficiency and effectiveness in service delivery rather than social mobilization. This emphasis has implications for how power and authority are exercised inside organizations, and with the communities they serve. This pressure may result in an NGO's sense of accountability to its values and these communities becoming less important. In Bangladesh, for example, this process of shifting accountability has seen the role of NGOs move from:

> ... promoting rights through class struggle to class harmony, privileged the sustainability of the institution over sustainability of the work on the ground or the local groups, and moved to a more elite leadership of civil society groups to produce a more assimilationist model, which appeases donors and doesn't threaten the state.

> (Syed and Hassan 1999: 127)

The requirements of the donors and the state imply certain types of accountability, which are not only privileged over accountability to the aid recipients, but in some cases can militate against it. The other related pressure is that the direction of accountability for the NGO is often defined by the demands of the 'project' itself, a central requirement of most donors either foreign or local. The project is time bound, with certain outcomes expected that lead to an impact in an idealistic and logical way. However, as we have seen in the case studies, empowerment may not easily lend itself to such logical processes. Even when an NGO is given the freedom to develop the programme, there is the pressure from donors on specific time-based expenditure targets and predicted outcomes, which if not met the NGO is often penalized. 'The reality is that they [NGOs] are in the grip of a neo-modernization algorithm that assumes projects *are* development. As their budgets rise … so they demand more and more projects on which to spend their money …' (Elliot 1987: 60).

There are exceptions, however, and these are instructive. From Chapter 5 the most successful NGOs programme in empowerment terms was that of the waste-pickers, whereby the NGO, SNDT avoided the notion of the 'project' all together, and managed to find donors that would accept institutional funding rather than project funding. Generally, however, donors seek certainty in the programmes they support, while the aid recipients are more uncertain as to their future and so they seek more flexibility in how they use the resources they receive, leading to tensions. The effect of the demand for more certainty from donors is that the source of funds can influence the direction and focus of NGO accountability to the donor, with upward shift of accountability and 'puppetization of NGOs' (Zaidi 1999: 264), or NGO sector becoming a 'shadow state' (Sen, S. 1999: 329). This trend can be seen in Bangladesh where a small number of very large NGOs seem to act as an oligarchy, while in India this occurs much less, and across many more contexts. The process that evolves is that a dependency-based, patron-client relationship emerges as a consequence of donor and state pressures. Combined with a lack of a formal representative framework, this leads to these oligarchic governance structures within NGOs, particularly in their relationship with their aid recipients. Michel's 'iron law of oligarchy', which argues that if unchecked, membership organizations will shift from democratic to oligarchic control (Michel, 1915 quoted in Fisher 1994), seems very apt for NGOs, particularly as they are non-membership organizations, and so there are fewer checks (Davis 1995). The weakness inherent in the governance structure of NGOs and their accountability pressures to donors and the state gives little support for the idea of them being natural empowerment agents; however, there has to be some linkage with the aid recipients for the NGO to be credible in its work: 'but most [NGO] leaders do depend on their claim of representation to sustain their organizational power over time so they have to represent some of the members to some degree some of the time' (Fox and Brown 1998: 22).

The results from the study, however, show that accountability is important for NGOs, but not in the ways that much of the literature discussed above perceives it; the literature tends to look at accountability to government and donors, and the broader issue of transparency, rather than the direction of accountability per se. While the Indian NGOs in the study talked about their accountability to the state and donors, particularly official donors, they tended to see their accountability in a complex way, highlighting values, the work, and their constituencies. The NGO accountability framework (Figure 3) posits that accountability to the 'values' and 'constituency' are directly related to the nature of the work of the NGO itself, and the accountability to the donor and the state is related to accessing the resources for, and legal requirements of, the NGO to undertake their work.

Accountability to values

All of the Indian NGO case studies placed accountability to their values as the most important form of accountability they had, and contrary to a lot of popular opinion and some literature, none of the NGOs surveyed saw themselves as being driven solely by funding contracts. Half of the NGOs in the study had not taken up funding offers, or had initiated the ending of funding relationships, on the basis that the conditions set by donors did not accord with their values. The problem these NGOs saw, though, is that in the first decade of the twenty-first century, while the amount of funding available was increasing, the range of sources of funding was narrowing, with a major shift to domestic sources. This shift presented a challenge to many of the NGOs of the priority of adherence to their values. The values of the case study NGOs were expressed in different ways among the group as they had different foci. Most of the NGOs' values were expressed in one way or another in their mission statement and they clearly articulated them in discussions. The origins of the values for these NGOs they saw as coming from a moral, or a religiously based ethic for some, and an altruistic notion of 'what is right' for others. None of them saw service provision as an end in itself, but as a way of achieving or meeting the aims of their values. These were generally expressed in terms of what the NGO aims to do in its work, or in terms of its relationship with its constituency and what it hopes to achieve with them. For example, SNDT's values were described in terms of 'justice and equality' for their constituency, the waste-pickers, which then had implications for both the organizational and staff behaviour in relation to the waste-pickers. For IDS in Dharwad, the values were also in terms of both staff and organizational behaviour of maintaining 'responsibility and integrity' in how they work. Other NGOs in the study saw their values in terms of the outcome for their aid recipients, which for most was empowerment and self-reliance. For example, in the case of KIDS it was anti-exploitation and women's rights for 'the poorer sections' of society. Related to these organizational values were the personal values of staff, which should reflect the organization's values. Generally these were expressed, not in instrumental terms, but rather in the relationship with the community they were working with, with common terms used such as 'partnership' or 'working in solidarity', supported by the notions of integrity and sincerity in how the work is undertaken. They felt then that these personal values should be imparted to the aid recipients. Many respondents saw the NGO staff as being central to imparting these values, and indicated that they had particular staff selection, development, and support programmes to ensure staff, and their approach to the work, reflected these values. As to whether this was also reflected in direct accountability mechanisms to the aid recipients, the results were mixed.

The issue that most of the participating NGOs had was the difficulty of having specific mechanisms of being accountable to their values. First, accountability to values can often be demonstrated in terms of programming decisions. For example, if a programme evolved in a direction not consistent with the organization's values of working with the poor then the staff should have responded and made the necessary programme changes. Second, accountability to values can be demonstrated through the aid recipients themselves, and how they responded to the NGO in terms of their support and involvement in the work. Finally, the most interesting indicator of accountability to values was the response of those who opposed a particular programme, and the reasons they gave. For example, if a wealthier group in the community complained to a government donor that they were being excluded from the programme on the grounds that it was favouring marginalized groups in the community, then this was a positive indication that the work was effective. While it is the Board's responsibility to ensure that an NGO is adhering to its values, it is the three mechanisms outlined above that reflected more closely the work on the ground, and provided a more immediate measure of an agency's accountability to their values, when these values related to empowerment or rights of the marginalized. The challenge is how this can be tracked on a day-to-day basis to avoid a gradual erosion of values, when there is a conflict of values, particularly with the values of the donor. Here the pressure to accept funding for certain purposes, such as the watershed programme in Karnataka described in Chapter 3, and the issues that arose, can have an effect on how an NGO sees its values in the day-to-day work.

The accountability of NGOs to their values in their relationship with the aid recipients, as well as how they developed the relationship with the donors, can be illustrated in how some agencies had rejected generous offers from donors for programmes which, on close analysis, were not in line with their values. In one case a donor wanted the NGO concerned, whose values were around alternative health issues and traditional medicine, to carry out a community awareness programme around health issues solely based on the existing formal health structure, rather than incorporating traditional practices. In another case World Bank funds were returned for a social forestry project, when it emerged that the project would promote policies that were not in the tribal people's best interests. For one NGO, the accountability to values was 'always the driving force, which they cannot allow to be diluted'. SNDT's mechanisms for accountability to its values were framed in terms of the personal link between the staff and the waste-pickers, and how the staff saw their work. SNDT rejected the notion of the NGO as being an 'outsider'; and the organization's values reflected the notion of equality of SNDT and its staff with the waste-pickers so that '[we] ... cannot talk of doing the work for the people; they do it for themselves' (quote from SNDT worker). This formulation of the staff motivation moved away from the notion of altruism towards one of solidarity. If this was the core value of the organization then accountability to its values were tied up with accountability to the community they were working with, and how that was exercised. SNDT had very strong and formal accountability mechanisms to the waste-pickers through their union, the KKPKP.

However, for most of the NGOs surveyed, the notion of accountability to their values was less clear. They saw their values being reflected in the work and less of a driving force per se. Nevertheless, while few NGOs had formal mechanisms to hold themselves to account to their values, or sanctions in place if they did not follow them, the majority could give clear instances where decisions were directed on the basis of these values, and choices appraised against them. They saw themselves as having a set of objectives, out of which a series of complex relationships emerged with donors, aid recipients and government. Here each has tried to influence the other in terms of organizational priorities and values. In all cases these relationships were negotiated, rather than being based on a strict client-patron relationship. Key to this was that the accountability to values was framed in terms of the communities the NGOs were working with. This way a linkage could be drawn with the accountability to the recipients, and how this panned out on a daily basis with the other accountability pressures these NGOs faced.

Values, however, can become eroded over time through organization growth, staff change, or changes in the preferences of donors or aid recipients. For most of the NGOs studied in this book, there were clear induction processes and staff selection criteria that attempted to inculcate and reflect the values. There was also a feeling that as an organization grew and the array of accountabilities became more complex, and the range and size of the communities they were working with also increased, it was harder to maintain the same level of accountability to values that one might find in a new or smaller organization. An example of changing donor/ government preferences is the emphasis in the early 2000s on the effectiveness of microfinance in poverty alleviation programmes. For local NGOs this led to a move away from the most marginalized groups, who have limited capacity for managing microfinance loans, to more 'entrepreneurial' sectors of the community who were able to show more immediate 'results'. In the case of KIDS, their major donor changed their aid preferences so that in the space of two years they moved from supporting a focus on violence against women to one of looking at the impact of globalization on the community. This resulted in some soul-searching as KIDS tried to maintain the donor relationship, and the focus on their key constituency, women as victims of gender-based violence. The question that arises is how an agency maintains a focus on its values, ensures that they are relevant, and that the work continues to be accountable to these values. Related to this is how the values enable these NGOs to be accountable to their aid recipients. Overall, for this group of NGOs in southern India, they saw the adherence to values as providing the clearest basis for accountability to the communities they were working with, and the basis for their empowerment work.

A related point from these case studies was that the values base of an organization was not something which was a given, but was in constant flux and tension with the often rapidly changing local context. For these NGOs it was the values that must be worked on, and the activities they were engaged in should be appraised against them. From the discussion with a range of NGOs it seemed that time, growth, and external influences resulted in some erosion of values. It can be argued that it is the larger, and very small and newer, NGOs who are most vulnerable to this trend. This was borne out with the rapid change to NGOs in the last few years when international donor support had declined, to be replaced with local government supported programmes with much tighter rules and different foci. This has caused issues among the NGOs in how they see the accountability to their values in a time of tighter and less flexible sources of resources, and the pressures and tensions that emerge when staff have to be laid off. These dilemmas that NGOs faced in how they asserted their values are linked to theories of power. It is the assertion of values with a particular group that can be an expression of power; if not in the Weberian notions of domination, then in Giddens' views of influencing the conduct of others. While the NGOs in this study argued that their approach to empowerment was an assertion of their values, their limited approach to being accountable to aid recipients indicated that this accountability was tightly bounded in terms of both the processes used, and the possible sanctions that could be used against the NGO. Because of NGOs' greater endowments in resources both physical and by virtue of their status, and their relative skill in negotiation, NGOs could exert power in these relationships. This resulted in their capacity for facilitating empowerment being compromised when dealing with disempowered people, especially poor women. Some NGOs could exert their influence over the women in a way that led to some level of dependency, thus limiting empowerment. While this group of Indian NGOs saw their values as their distinguishing feature in line with much of the literature (inter alia Lissner 1977; Gerard 1983; Fowler 1996; Edwards and Sen 2000), the real test was how much these values could be eroded by other accountability pressures, and more importantly, how these values were reflected in the accountability relationship the NGO had with its aid recipients.

Accountability to the aid recipients

The forms of accountability the NGOs surveyed have to the communities they work with is detailed in Chapter 5. Those that showed the greatest level of formality in their accountability processes to the aid recipients had the strongest empowerment outcomes. Most of the NGOs surveyed saw some level of accountability to the aid recipients as an important aspect of their work, and this was played out at a practical level, usually with NGO staff and management having regular meetings with the SHGs, in order to gauge the relevance and usefulness of their interventions. While Fox and Brown (1998) argue that these more or less informal accountability processes can be quite powerful in establishing NGO legitimacy, I would argue from the findings of this study, that informal accountability processes at best link the NGO instrumentally (that is, through its work) but not structurally or politically to the recipients. The evidence was that it was the more structural (formal) links that delivered stronger empowerment outcomes, in line with Joshi and Moore (2000) who argue that the presence of formal processes establishes a right for the aid recipients to claim services and the like from the NGO, and it is this 'right' that is the basis for empowerment.

Many of the NGOs in this study, such as IDS and MYRADA, dealt with the issue of accountability through formal structures such as federations rather than direct accountability processes. Federation structures per se were not a source of accountability, but rather, the downward accountability was related to how these structures were used. NGOs that had formal, semi-formal, or informal account-ability mechanisms all grouped the SHGs into federations, but their roles varied considerably. For example, even though MYRADA used a federation structure there was little evidence that it was used as a mechanism of 'downward' account-ability, while both the union in the case of the SNDT, and the federation in the case of Grama Vikas, were consciously used as a mechanism for being accountable to the recipients. Federation structures are not necessarily an accountability mechan-ism, but more used for participation, devolution of management, and programme sustainability mechanisms (Howes 1997). The role of the federations, or what MYRADA calls People's Organizations, was a functional one, which was involved in practical matters such as income-generation and savings programmes, and dealt mainly with livelihood matters that affected the members of the group, while the NGO was involved in advocacy and rights work. In neither case, however, was it clear to what extent the federations influence the NGOs strategic direction, which some NGOs argue is their preserve as public benefit organizations, with no place for recipients in these processes.

NGOs did not like to be bound to a particular and restricted membership, such as SNDT's waste-picker programme and KKPKP, as the members quite naturally will seek to advance their own interests. Few of the NGOs in the study had members from the recipient communities on their Boards, as they were afraid that political forces may emerge and hijack the NGO's values or priorities for more sectional interests. Or alternatively having community representatives on their Boards can weaken the NGO's effectiveness through conflicting interests developing among various community representatives. SNDT, which had the strongest and most formal mechanism of 'downward' accountability, tended to manage these tensions through their involvement in decision-making as equals with their waste-pickers who were the majority of the Board of KKPKP. They preferred this approach to having a dichotomy of 'insiders' and 'outsiders', with the waste-pickers being treated as the outsiders when it came to Board processes. For SNDT active inclusion was an integral part of a just way to acting with integrity and of gaining true legitimacy with the recipient community. SNDT had the power to reject directions from the waste-pickers on matters of values. For example, communalism is an issue whereby the waste-pickers, due to their caste status, could favour a more communalist approach in certain social situations, while SNDT, being part of a women's university, had values that were strongly related to pluralism, diversity and non-violence, and they made this quite clear to the waste-pickers. The same principle could be applied to the issue of expansion to other groups in society. For SNDT the issue of expansion of the constituency was difficult and sensitive, but for them it was one that should not be imposed but argued with the waste-pickers' union as equals. With the advent of SWaCH and the support of the Municipal Corporation, the KKPKP had to broaden its views with regard to membership in any case, and accepted other non-union members into SWaCH.

In other cases the accountability to the recipients became important because the NGO concerned had grown in size over time, or its focus changed. In order to stay in touch and remain relevant, these NGOs felt that mechanisms that brought them closer to the recipients were important. The Development Academy was changing rapidly in the early 2000s, and it introduced some accountability changes to bring it closer to the recipients, with two local SHG representatives on the Board (out of seven). They also used the existing Grain Banks (village community-based organizations organized by the Academy) to take on a greater role in managing the range of Academy programmes in a particular village, and also to provide valuable feedback to the staff who worked with those villages. This, however, was the exception, with most NGOs not having a clear conception of their aid recipients being their constituency. This book has argued that this must be a key consideration if empowerment programmes are to be effectively directed to disempowered groups in a community.

While these NGOs all stated that they aimed to focus on the poor, few went beyond a generalized statement such as this to identify a more specific group of their aid recipients that might be seen as a constituency. Those that did focus on a particular group, such as SNDT with waste-picker women, the Development Academy or Grama Vikas with mainly *dalit* women) had procedures and practices in place to ensure that programmes were directed to these particular groups. Other NGOs' representatives such as IDS conceded that the level of constituency focus had weakened over time, with less focus on the most marginalized groups, and they now had fewer processes to assess whether these groups were being reached. MYRADA, on the other hand, left the selection of beneficiaries to the villagers themselves, resulting, according to the evidence, in a poorer outcome in reaching the very poor or the most marginalized groups relative to other NGOs in the study. This approach of MYRADA in the study area seemed to reflect a rather naïve view of village politics. It ignored the maxim that those in power will attempt to capture benefits for themselves with forms of rent-seeking behaviour. A more realistic approach for MYRADA in these communities would have involved an assessment of who the disadvantaged were on the basis of whether they were food stamp recipients (the most common form of welfare), and other criteria such as their assets, caste and education; and only then from that list undertake a joint process of selection on the basis of need.

For these NGOs the idea of a constituency focus, based on a generic category of aid recipients such as the very poor, is weak for two reasons: firstly, NGOs generally lacked capacity in social analysis, and so failed to give sufficient attention to complex socio-political issues; and secondly, donor funding patterns have changed, so these donors are now less concerned with marginalized groups such as *dalits* or poverty reduction per se, which was the focus of the 1980s. The result was that with the Indian Government being the major donor, the focus has moved quite a way from the marginalized to the 'rural poor' as a more general category. There was also a more fragmented approach in donor priorities (either government or INGOs), with specific issues such as environment, microfinance and gender-based violence all becoming the focus of donor attention. While these issues are vital in any development programme, this change in focus meant that NGOs ended up being reduced to just implementing activities, with social analysis and the subsequent strategic planning in decline. The effect of these changes in aid direction was to fragment recipient groups, thus weakening the concept of a constituency of aid recipients for an NGO, and it also ran the risk of leaving out the most marginalized groups. This is important as I have argued that there should be more formal mechanisms of accountability to those an NGO is working with, but this is difficult if the aid recipients are spread among a number of social groups.

Two issues regarding NGO accountability have emerged, and they can be summarized simply as the 'how' and the 'who' of accountability. So far much of the discussion has dealt with the question of 'how' accountability should occur. The question of 'who' the NGO should be accountable to relates to their values and mission and how they see their aid recipients as a constituency. While account-ability in the case of the Indian NGOs this book covers can be measured by the range and types of relationships the NGO has with the self-help groups, the accountability to an NGO constituency more broadly can be argued to be the 'reach' of a particular programme to marginalized groups, reflecting a view that accountability can be approached through the work of the NGO. This account-ability to a broader constituency can be in conflict with the accountability to a particular group, who quite naturally would like to maximize the benefits of the programme to themselves, rather than see a programme expand to other disadvan-taged people or groups. This is a juggling act that NGOs have to manage: on the one hand they have to be responsive and accountable to the group with which they are working, and give power to that group. On the other hand, they have to be aware of and responsive to that part of their broader constituency that they are not reaching. The upshot of this dilemma is that effective empowerment involves giving the groups greater direct control over the programme, with the perverse effect of limiting the scope of the programme in terms of a broader constituency or potential aid recipients.

For example, while SNDT was directed more by the constituency of waste-pickers than most, it was also involving its staff in extending the reach to other waste-pickers, and debating with the established groups the importance of this move. This level of growth and expansion is possible in a union structure (which the waste-pickers have) as all members benefit by expansion, because their primary focus is on collective rights, and so strength in numbers is important. Where the focus is on credit and savings facilities (with material benefits for individuals), new members who join may be regarded as free-loading on the work done by the established members who may resist newcomers joining. Indeed, this occurred with KKPKP, who insisted that new members pay 'back fees' from the year union started – in this case up to ten years – as there was a material benefit in the form of subsidy involved. Likewise, there may also be opportunistic behaviour from the privileged groups who have power to exclude those more disempowered, and as we have seen, this may be one reason for the relatively poor results for some NGOs in selecting the most marginalized. The role of the donor (government of INGO) likewise cannot be excluded in the discussion of NGO accountability to values and aid recipients, as NGOs have to manage an accountability relationship with their donors.

Accountability to donors

Accountability to the donor (the source of resources for the NGO) is complex and can affect how an NGO works to its values and is accountable to its aid recipients. The Indian NGOs in this study had a range of donors from whom they accessed resources, and in recent years the set of donors had narrowed to a greater emphasis on local Indian donors by way of federal and state government programmes. In general, the donors fell into two main groups, the government (usually state governments, but sometimes central and local governments); and secondly, private NGOs – mostly INGOs from abroad, who may or may not have accessed government funds for the activities in their own countries. There were no clear characteristics of the relationship with either group of donors. Some government departments were easier to deal with than others, which was also true of international and local NGO donors, but generally NGOs found the shift to local donors more difficult to manage, given a shift in focus and a move to more provider contracting models.

The main concern of all donors was financial accountability, followed by accountability to the agreed objectives and activities of the programme. In some cases accountability to the government's priorities was very direct, in which case the NGO was effectively a contractor. None of the government programmes that these NGOs were involved with favoured approaches that promoted accountability to the aid recipients. For national and local governments, social mobilization (and empowerment) is at best a lesser priority and at worst an illegal or threatening activity (Sen, S. 1999), with most Indian states having rules against NGOs being involved in what they refer to as 'instigation', or advocacy to seek change in policy or even push for the enforcement of existing government policy. There was also pressure for rigorous (and expensive) financial audits. The Council for Advancement of People's Action and Rural Technology (CAPART), a major funder, was a difficult agency to deal with. In the past there had been audits of its programmes, which identified irregularities including fraudulent activities, such as payments to non-existent NGOs. As a result, CAPART had tightened its accountability and verification procedures to the extent of instituting a programme of checks with the District Administrator, and the Central Bureau of Investigation, to verify the bona fides of the NGO finances and the relevance of the work. Before 2000 these government donors had little effect on the direction of the work, but more recently the government programmes have changed their criteria, which has altered the direction of NGO work. The tougher accountability and verification processes did lead to considerable delays in funding; while at the same time providing opportunities for corruption from officials. Examples of delays in payment from government departments, such as KWDP as detailed in Chapter 3, has led to a cash flow crisis in a number of the NGOs, resulting in them laying off staff. In addition, some programmes were asking for a 10 per cent deposit of the value of the programme as a Bank Guarantee, and as a result many NGOs were very reluctant to participate in some government programmes, but they often had little choice. Participating in microfinance programmes supported by government development banks, such as NABARD and SIDBI, runs the risk of the NGO becoming a form of commission agent for the banks, in which the NGO bears the risk while the banks remained safe. As we have seen in Chapter 3, Chinyard, with its microfinance programme, is an example of an NGO bearing a large risk.

Some donors were more interventionist in the programming of the activities and small agencies were at the mercy of the donor. In KIDS' case funding was withdrawn due to strategic changes in the donor organization, who would only support a certain type of programmes with specific strategic intent such as globalization, when previously it was focusing on gender-based violence. These changes in focus (often at relatively short notice) in strategic direction of INGO donors had dire effects on the smaller NGOs they had been supporting. The emerging trend was that INGO donors were becoming more hands-on and operational in their approach, and some were using local NGOs effectively as contractors for their global advocacy campaigns. This more hands-on donor intervention can be positive; for example, UNDP had suggested the Development Academy set up a co-ordinating mechanism when it noted that the Academy's projects were all independent of each other, even within the same village. Likewise, many INGOs provided an advisory service for evaluation and other planning support for their smaller NGOs partners. The advantage of these mechanisms was that they could be separated from the direct programme management accountability mechanisms of the donor. This 'non-funding support' was seen as an important part of programming for many INGOs, but they seem to overstate how the local NGOs saw it: neither the funding or non-funding support of INGOs to KKPKP was mentioned in the ten-year report of the waste-picker union (Chikaramane and Narayan 2005). The relationship of local NGOs with INGO donors was more mixed than with the local government donors. On the one hand, INGOs were more supportive, and allowed a large degree of flexibility, such as was the case with SNDT, Grama Vikas, or IDS. On the other hand they could affect the local NGOs' strategic directions, and even their very existence. The relationship an NGO had with its donors, and the influence donors had on NGO work, could have an effect on the NGO's accountability to its values and aid recipients.

Another way donors can weaken NGO accountability to their values and aid recipients, is through the promotion of what some might call 'development fashions'. At the village level many of these 'fashions' seemed not to be relevant to day-to-day life – such as NGO work on globalization, or free trade. While clearly links can be made to the livelihood of villagers and these global issues, the links may be not be very evident to a very poor marginalized woman socially isolated by her gender, caste, and class. Some of the 'fashions' can seem to be seductive particularly if they are linked to funding: 'carrots being foreign funding/assignments around "fashionable terms" which can result in you being caught in a trap. The lingo of globalization can be marginalizing. You need to either counter it or cope with it' (SNDT staff). Other examples of this problem were microfinance and natural resource management, both of which were undergoing an unprecedented boom throughout the 1990s and 2000s. Most of the NGOs surveyed that worked in rural areas were involved with both of these issues, and so microfinance was a necessary entry point for most NGO activities, mainly because most poor and marginalized households did not have secure incomes, and were dependent on high-cost credit for their daily living. By introducing schemes to reduce the cost of credit, NGOs gained access to communities, and from that access raised awareness or delivered a range of other services. The access also enabled them to engage with the community on what the NGO saw as priority strategic issues that affected the aid recipients' lives, such as alcoholism, gender-based violence and caste discrimination.

The problem, however, with the rapid growth in microfinance support from donors and government financial institutions was that the microfinance programmes themselves became ends at the expense of other social programmes, and even developed into forms of debt traps. The government of India aimed to increase the number of self-help groups from 531,000 to 1.4 million by 2004 (*The Indian Express*, October 21, 2001: 8). In order to secure this type of donor finance, NGOs may have to develop activities that move them away from their core values and programmes, or from their prime constituency.

Government-sponsored SHG programmes

Stree Shakti is the largest government-sponsored SHG programme, with a target of 120,000 self-help groups reaching more than 2,000,000 women. These groups would be organized by the *anganwadi* (pre-school) teachers, with the NGOs training the teachers in self-help group formation. Such a programme can disrupt existing groups as these new groups will receive a direct government grant of seed money. The second scheme is *Swarna Jayanthi Gram Rosger Stree Yojim*, a central government scheme aimed at those people below the poverty line joining self-help groups organized by NGOs, in which after a qualifying period they would be eligible for a loan of Rs250,000 for the purchase of assets such as cattle. One-third of this loan would be in the form a subsidy payable at the end of the first loan cycle. The aim is to reach 100 SHGs per district and ultimately see a total of 1.4 million SHGs nationally. The third scheme, *Swashakti*, is a World Bank financed programme through the state government in which no finance would be made available, but funding would be available for NGOs to cover staff costs and training.

These microfinance schemes have both advantages and disadvantages for NGOs and existing SHGs: they were attractive to NGOs, but as mentioned above could have the effect of diverting NGOs resources from their main activities. However, strong NGOs, such as Grama Vikas or MYRADA, took advantage of schemes such as *Swashakti* to cover some staff costs. In some cases these national programmes even helped NGOs focus on poor and marginalized groups. For example, the

Swashakti programme, which had a strong poverty focus, targeted villages according to their sex ratio. The sex ratio was regarded as a good indicator of women marginalization and disempowerment, and within those low sex ratio villages, the programme targeted below poverty line (BPL) women, women with low literacy rates, and those from the scheduled castes and scheduled tribes. Accessing this programme meant that at least those NGOs that took advantage of *Swashakti* funding were reaching communities according to strong indicators of poverty and marginalization. Accountability to the donor steered some NGO programmes away from their target groups, but there are other cases where some government anti-poverty programmes (usually with international donor support) had the effect of focusing the NGO onto those they would see as their primary constituency.

Accountability to the state

In India the state, at all levels, plays a key role in the regulation of NGOs with a range of procedures and monitoring mechanisms to ensure NGO accountability. Indian governments insist on two things. The first is that NGOs are financially transparent, and the second is that they do not enter the field of politics, which naturally has many grey areas. The NGOs in the study did not see these requirements as particularly onerous, and none of them had major difficulties with the government requirements. However, as the history of Indian NGOs covered in Chapter 2 has shown, these requirements give an indication of the level of suspicion and sometimes hostility from the state, and the laws before the federal government could see this situation change quickly (Jalali 2008).

National level: As outlined in Chapter 2, at the national level, the Union Government had a series of regulations and requirements under the Tax Act and the Foreign Contributions Regulation Act – FCRA (the latter Act regulates those NGOs which are registered to receive foreign funding). NGOs receiving foreign funding were regularly checked by the Central Bureau of Investigation, and had to establish three years of successful operation before being eligible to receive foreign funding, and their local programme had to be verified by the District Collector (the most senior government official in a district). While these regulations have not led to any major problems for these NGOs, they have led to considerable delays in implementing NGO programmes. The regulations also carry the threat of suspension of FCRA approval if NGOs engage in certain types of advocacy. Generally, NGOs avoid these threats by garnering the *indirect* support of individuals and/or representative organizations in their campaigns. An example of this is the Narmada Dam advocacy coalition in which the 'front person' is a well-known writer, Arundhati Roy, who has no identifiable NGO connections.

State level: at the state level the extent of regulation varied across the country. In general, these NGOs surveyed did not encounter major problems but the Karnataka State Government did monitor NGOs for involvement in 'instigation'. There were grey areas, however, such as anti-alcohol campaigns that effected government revenue; as the government could not be seen to be supportive of alcohol consumption as such, these campaigns were often not seen to be 'instigation', but the risk remained. On the whole, NGOs such as KIDS and IDS that undertook limited advocacy campaigns ensured that they were concerned with upholding existing laws (for example, child rights, alcohol abuse, and gender-based violence) rather than challenging legislation. Also, the NGO-sponsored federations (in the case of IDS and Grama Vikas) took on an advocacy role as representative organizations, which to some extent protected the NGO.

Local level: At the local level there are two main mechanisms by which the NGOs are accountable. First, through the changes to the FCRA in 2000 the local administrator or Collector had to provide a statement verifying the bona fides of the NGO, and ensured its work was not against local government policy. At the *gram panchayat* or village government level there were no formal accountability mechanisms, therefore different NGOs related to the *gram panchayats* in different ways. IDS, for instance, saw it as crucial to regularly brief the *gram panchayat* members about their work in order to avoid conflict, and they regularly informed the Sarpanch (village secretary) of all of their work, and stayed in touch with the ward members. Some NGOs, such as MYRADA, set up parallel mechanisms whereby a planning group, separate to the *gram panchayat*, is the consultative forum for MYRADA's work. Overall, however, there was some ambivalence about the role of village government among the NGOs surveyed. Only one NGO *felt* accountable to the *gram panchayat*', with most seeing the real point of accountability as being with the District Collector who had to approve any NGO's presence and work in the community. Accountability of the NGOs to the state (at various levels) had little impact on these NGOs' ability to be accountable to their values and their constituencies. In fact, the regulations against advocacy provided an opportunity for greater direct participation in advocacy on local issues by the constituency through their representative organizations established by the NGOs.

Conclusion

All of the NGOs interviewed saw themselves as being accountable bodies, with the majority seeing their accountability to their values as being their primary concern and motivation. In turn they believed their values were expressed through their work. However, few of the NGOs had explicit mechanisms for being accountable to their values. It is arguable that this lack of accountability mechanisms to values leaves them vulnerable, as those accountability pressures that require specific mechanisms can inadvertently be given a priority, and be seen to dominate or dilute their values. Few of the NGOs studied had major difficulties with accountability to the donors, either Indian government or foreign donors. However, a major concern arising with SHG programmes is that they are with predominately savings and credit groups with an emphasis on financial concerns. While accessing inexpensive credit is of importance for women, a number of the NGOs put an overriding emphasis on credit as an 'end' in itself, either explicitly or implicitly. This resulted in prioritizing the donor, whether it was a bank, government wholesaler, or another NGO, while diminishing the accountability to either the NGO's values or their aid recipients.

While the requirements of donors in general have tightened over recent years, none of the NGOs surveyed found them either unfair or onerous: 'the donor has the right to receive information and ask questions, but they cannot tell us what to do' (was one response). In the past INGO donors tended to have a hands-off approach, and base the relationship on trust or what was referred to as a 'guilt thing' from a colonial legacy. In retrospect, this approach is arguably irresponsible, and following a number of scandals, is slowly changing, and according to some of the respondents it is for the better. Fowler (2000b), Edwards (1999a) and others argue that northern donors have undue control over southern NGOs, but this view is not borne out in practice for these and others NGOs in India, where it would seem that Indian government funders are wielding much of the control. In relation to INGO donors, as we have seen, half of the group of NGOs interviewed had explicitly avoided new donor relationships, and terminated or rejected donor funding on the grounds that the grant conditions were contrary to their values. In addition, while the other NGOs were less specific, they indicated that they would only enter new donor relationships with some caution. However, the agencies that were most vulnerable to donor control were the smaller agencies with less than ten staff, and usually dependent on a single donor for specific activities rather than a broader programme. The evidence indicates that, except for a small number of exceptions, the relationship between INGO and the local NGO is not a strict patron-client relationship; nor, however, is it a partnership based on equality. Rather the relationship is built on a series of negotiations on what are perceived to be the common goals. Accountability from the donor's perspective, in general, is to see that their funds are spent efficiently and effectively for that common goal. From the local NGO's point of view, it was often the in-kind contribution from donors that was as important as the funding, and represented the core of the relationship. In general this type of support was not forthcoming from local, particularly government donors, and thus could emerge as a problem with the recent shift to government donors.

Accountability to the aid recipients was the area where the NGOs interviewed had the most difficulty. While most agreed that it was very important for programme effectiveness, they did not wish to become beholden to a particular, and arguably, narrower constituency, when their mission was to a broader section of a community. While several of the NGOs had mechanisms for accountability to the aid recipients, or were developing mechanisms, only SNDT saw this level of accountability as a central function of their institution. Most of the others would prefer the term 'participation' rather than 'representation' in the strict accountability sense. The NGOs did not relate their accountability to the aid recipients in terms of their overall objective of empowerment. While none were surprised with the finding that accountability to the aid recipients was a significant variable in empowerment, the overall view was that an increased move in accountability to them would weaken the NGO's control over the programme. It could also create tensions and divert the NGO away from a broader group in a community to a narrower 'membership' base.

Further work is also required in the area of programme management theory to identify mechanisms for the development of formal or semi-formal accountability structures to provide the NGO's recipients with a greater sense of ownership (and therefore power) in the programme while maintaining the flexibility to expand their work to new communities. The example of SNDT and Grama Vikas indicated that this was possible. Joshi and Moore (2000), however, caution that it is an exceptional organization that can do this. Nevertheless, this is an important area for policy work if empowerment programmes are to meet their real objectives of the poor being able to challenge power relationships at all levels in their lives.

7   Conclusion

Introduction

This book has identified two broad trends in NGO work in India, which are in tension with each other. For southern India in particular, the economic success of the region, and the related drop in the headline measures of poverty, have resulted in international aid agencies withdrawing from the southern states, with their former work in rural development and poverty alleviation being largely taken over by both federal and state instrumentalities. These government agencies have less flexible approaches, and a broader development agenda for rural areas, than the sharper focus on poverty alleviation and empowerment that INGOs had. These domestic government agencies also tend to follow the purchaser-provider model of government contracting for service provision, whereby the NGO is more of an agent for government programmes than offering up its own programmes for their support as they did with INGOs. This change has naturally led to a narrowing of the control that these local NGOs hitherto had. As discussed in Chapter 3, this has led to difficulties for the NGOs in this study; they had to dismiss staff and look to different funding options as they managed a fairly rapid change.

The second trend has been that since the early to mid-1990s Indian NGOs have had a stronger focus on empowerment of poor women in their development work, and have adopted the savings and credit self-help group model to achieve this. Generally there has been a strong focus on social transformation and empowerment as a path to reducing poverty and marginalization among rural and urban women. This book has looked at this trend and identified some features of how NGOs work with marginalized women to achieve stronger empowerment outcomes. Strong empowerment for poor women was linked to the NGOs spending more time (in terms of years) with the women's self-help groups; and having stronger and more formal accountability relationships with these SHGs, who were the aid recipients. In the early 2000s local NGOs in Southern India were grappling with the conflicting implications of these trends. Experience suggested that if these NGOs were to be true to their values, they had to invest more time and effort in engaging with the marginalized women they were working with to be effective. However, the local NGOs' traditional resource base from the INGOs was being replaced by government programmes that contracted local NGOs as delivery agents for service provision, thus creating a dilemma for them. This chapter will summarize some of these findings, and look to ways forward for NGOs in India, which will have resonance with local NGOs in other rapidly developing countries. This will look at how they can approach and resource their work, so that the empowerment work can be strengthened and advanced.

Indian NGOs

Since independence NGOs have played an important role in India's development; over this time government relations have alternated between times of mutual suspicion and hostility, to periods of high levels of co-operation with NGOs taking a central role in the development agenda. After a period of co-operation in the 1950s followed by hostility and suspicion through the 1980s into the 1990s, by the early 2000s NGOs were more respected by government, and were having a more central role in the nation's development, as evidenced by increased funding though government programmes. This shift in the approach of government to NGOs coincided with a number of political and economic trends that started in the 1980s but accelerated in the 1990s. The spectacular growth of the Indian economy in the first decade of the 2000s, together with this new rapport with NGOs, has meant the government can resource much of its own development agenda using local NGOs more than hitherto possible, while at the same time international donors, both official and INGOs, are rapidly withdrawing.

These changes have meant that the Indian polity has had to manage the competing forces of globalization and modernization of the economy, and the emergence of a strong, mostly urban-based, middle class; as well as a strong religio-nationalist movement, part of which is based in the rural heartland, and challenges much of the modernization that has been occurring. The government's response to these competing trends has been to invest in rural areas and ensure the benefits of growth would reach many of these rural communities. The problem that governments faced was that they were poorly equipped to deliver services to the rural communities, and so the use of existing local NGOs to deliver these services made a lot of sense. As a result Indian government agencies invested heavily in NGO programmes. The effect of these changes has been two-fold: firstly, government favoured larger, often urban-based NGOs that had the capacity and experience in delivering government programmes; and secondly, local NGOs who were not in a position to take advantage of these government programmes, or wished to continue their empowerment work, had to re-scale their programmes to reflect their changed resource base, or seek alternative sources of support (see Chapter 3). The challenge with these changes was that there were fewer incentives for NGOs to continue empowerment work directly with marginalized groups and it also made it harder for them to look at processes for being accountable for their work to those groups.

NGOs and empowerment

From the empirical work with the 15 case study NGOs in Southern India, there are two principal findings: empowerment from the perspective of poor women is primarily related to improvements in their personal agency, the choices they can make and how they can act on them. However, there needs to be further work on how this has affected gender relations in the household, as any changes in this domain seemed to be weak. The second finding is that the nature of the accountability relationship (in terms of formal processes) of NGOs to the women's groups they work with played a key role in securing strong empowerment outcomes. These findings support the view that empowerment for the poor and marginalized is less about access to material resources and outcomes, and more about access to choices and decision-making that poor women have in both their household and community life. Central to these findings is the idea that empowerment is not an absolute condition, but rather a relative one. While it may be difficult to conceptualize degrees of empowerment, these results support the theories of empowerment (i.e. personal agency) derived mainly from the field of community psychology (e.g. Riger 1993). The processes that led to this type of empowerment can provide useful pointers to effective poverty alleviation strategies, and ways of working with marginalized communities in development practice more broadly.

The community psychology framework for empowerment focuses on individual self-esteem and confidence, which in terms of development practice enables marginalized groups, particularly women, to assert themselves in a much wider range of social and political domains in their family and community lives. The research also suggests that one of the 'domains' from which self-confidence and assertiveness can emerge and be applied more broadly, is in the accountability relationship the poor have with the agency facilitating their empowerment – often NGOs, but they can also be government agencies, or less commonly, private organizations such as banks or consulting companies. The importance of this finding is that it supports a view that empowerment is not something that is provided, but rather is inherent in the relationship between the organization and the communities it is working with. This view of empowerment being related to personal agency, and its relationship with the 'downward' accountability mechanisms of the organization (in this case NGOs) to the intended beneficiaries, has not been a strong focus in development discourse and practice to date.

Measuring agency

The methodology outlined in Chapter 5 focuses on women's own narratives of the important changes that had occurred in their lives, which were then put into an empowerment framework. This framework involved sorting responses into broad 'domains' and ranking them, from which a statistical analysis was made. This methodology can be adapted for assessing a range of development interventions, as the open-ended approaches used to gather data tend to bring out key issues in the relevance of particular approaches. The methodology has limitations, as it has an interpretive dimension, it requires careful training of enumerators to ensure consistent interpretations of responses and coding, and so large-scale comparisons may not yield useful results. The methodology is, however, very useful for longitudinal studies or smaller-scale comparative work, where fewer enumerators would be involved.

The change the women from the self-help groups reported most closely identified with, was the notion of personal agency. This change was articulated as an increase of self-esteem due to both the greater range of choices they had, and their increased capacity to act on those choices. As discussed in Chapter 5, these choices were incremental in nature, and ranged from the relatively straightforward capacity to go out of the house and interact with people outside the immediate family, to broader notions of engaging in civic processes in the village, and making autonomous decisions about their personal lives and influencing others in the family. These findings support a variation of Kabeer's empowerment theory, where she argues that empowerment is a combination of an increase in access to resources, material outcomes and personal agency (Kabeer 1999a). Community psychology theory, however, relates empowerment to the self-esteem, confidence and assertiveness that an expansion of an individual's choices and capacity for action brings (Campbell and Jovchelovitch 2000; Speer 2000); that is, empowerment is primarily about the expansion of personal agency, with access to resources being less of an outcome of empowerment. The resources, however, do serve to provide a foundation for continuing the process of empowerment of the individual.

This finding from the research varies from Kabeer's theory relating to resources and outcomes. The results pointed to a virtuous circle; that is, when women's groups engaged with facilitating NGOs, enhanced agency led to greater access to resources, leading to more agency and so on. In practical terms, the greater level of confidence and assertiveness of the women in a particular community meant they were able to gain greater access to social, political, as well as public services, and economic and other resources. They could do this by virtue of their capacity to demand these resources from a range of providers; and it was the access to these resources that then enabled the women to participate more broadly in other domains that affected their lives. The key resource that the group members identified with, however, was not so much the material benefits, but rather the social resource in the form of the support from the self-help group to which they belonged. This finding, that the group itself provides a resource for individual empowerment, is in line with the view that empowerment has a collective dimension and that it can only occur in a social context (Speer 2000). It also gives weight to Giddens' (1979) argument that power has a collective dimension and is only exercised in a collective framework (see Chapter 2). The tension identified by Riger (1993), that the solidarity and interdependence of a group may be threatened by individual empowerment (and the related increase in personal autonomy), was not found in the results from the group surveys. There was no evidence that individual empowerment was a major problem or a cause of group failure. This may well be because the target groups were relatively poor, and needed to maintain the solidarity the group brought them for a longer period of time.

Generally, in Indian village life, women are disempowered in many respects: they are excluded from public decision-making spaces; they are not part of village associational life; and generally, are not part of political life in terms of village meetings, and this was certainly the case in the case study communities. This exclusion was not only gender-based, but in many areas it was also caste-based, where *dalits* and tribal people were at times excluded from physical amenities such as wells, temples and the like. The research found that through the self-help groups these marginalized women gained access to these amenities. For them disempowerment was the denial of access to these very basic domains of power, while empowerment was gaining access not only to these but also to new domains of power (Vijayalakshmi 2001). One reason for the strength and cohesion of the SHGs in this study is that the very poor women had access to few other alternative formations and networks outside the home due to the chronic lack of access to power in their personal and social lives. The work of the NGO provided poor women with an opportunity to be part of a social grouping – the SHG itself. This level of social exclusion referred to above may not have been felt by wealthier women, or those who lived in different social contexts, who may have had alternative social groupings to join. One area for further research is to look at the differences in perceptions of empowerment from different wealth and status groups in society. Anecdotal evidence from the narratives of the women seemed to indicate that the more marginalized groups in society (such as *dalits*) with more restricted choices, saw empowerment most strongly in agency terms, rather than material terms. This provides useful information to guide the focus of future development programmes to the very poor and ensure the stability of SHGs. The results also pointed to disempowerment as being a consequence of social marginalization as much as, if not more than material deprivation. Poverty in this context was related to a lack of access to decision-making, and the associated lack of capacity for the poor to act autonomously.

The practical implication was that empowerment programmes that fostered choice, decision-making, personal autonomy, and control, were more likely to address issues of social marginalization than solely economic programmes. This is not to say that economic programmes should be ignored, but rather approaches that foster autonomy and decision-making within constituent groups are required if social benefits, in terms of empowerment, are to be gained. Traditionally, NGOs were seen as being well-suited to perform the role of facilitator in these empowering processes and this research supports the view that by facilitating women to work together in groups, NGOs can enable the social norms of gender, caste and other factors of exclusion to be challenged. At the same time it also allowed women to access new physical and social (decision-making) domains in their lives. However, there are some caveats on how NGOs can perform this role effectively.

NGOs as empowerment intermediaries

NGOs are commonly used by donors and other funding bodies as agents for the empowerment for very poor and marginalized communities in developing countries. Other non-NGO development agencies, either government or private (such as banks), tend not to focus on the very poor mainly because of the high transaction costs involved in terms of the agencies' time for what are seen as relatively small outcomes. NGOs, on the other hand, work with the poor and marginalized because of their values – inter alia, service, altruism, and/or a desire for a fair or just world. As values-based organizations, NGOs see their motivation as being a reflection of their values (for a public benefit) both in the work they engage in, and how this work is undertaken. For many NGOs the promotion of empowerment of the poor and marginalized is a consequence of their values base. The changes that happened in India in the early 2000s where the funding support moved from international donors to mainly Indian government sources, which had an emphasis on broader service delivery rather than empowering the poor, threatened the capacity of NGOs to undertake empowerment work, at least on a broad scale.

While NGOs can act as facilitators in the empowerment process, the case studies demonstrated that the results were not uniform across the group of NGOs in this study, in how the members of the SHGs were empowered. When these differences were examined two factors emerged that were found to be significant in affecting the NGOs' capacity to affect empowerment outcomes: the period for which the SHG had been meeting; and the accountability of the NGO itself to the group. To recap the discussion from Chapter 6: first; the number of years a group spends together is important as it enabled women to build confidence and trust to take power and responsibility within the SHG, make choices, and take action. This issue of the period NGOs engaged with SHGs was contentious, as there is pressure on NGOs both from INGO and government funders to limit their engagement with particular groups to a specific time-period in order to expand their reach to new communities. Some donors had gone as far as developing templates for SHG engagement so they could withdraw within a certain time period, often as little as three years. These tight timescales were counterproductive, as there were poor results in terms of both the empowerment of members, or whether the SHG was able to sustain itself, as both can take time for marginalized groups. This dilemma can lead to NGOs focusing their support to those groups in society who can show early results, such as those who may be better off in a particular community, or have already have had NGO interactions, thus excluding the marginalized. While such an instrumental approach to engaging with SHGs can show early but superficial changes, not only would it be unsustainable, but more importantly it would move the focus away from the poor in these communities.

Accountability

The second finding, and the one this book is mainly concerned with, is that the accountability mechanisms the NGO has with the group can itself be empowering for the group and its members (Day and Klein 1987). That is, to be able to hold somebody to account is to exercise power over them. Because NGOs are non-membership bodies the process of accountability is not as clear-cut as if they were membership bodies. Nevertheless, among the case study NGOs there were examples in which the NGOs had mechanisms for being accountable to the groups they were working with, that allowed (some) power to be exercised over them by the aid recipients. The two key lessons were that the more formal the process the greater the level of empowerment, and furthermore, that empowerment is strongly identified with personal agency. This has implications for NGO practice, and it affects their role as public benefit organizations. NGOs in their work with poor and marginalized communities are in quite a powerful position as they are bodies over which the groups they work with have little power, given there are few alternatives for the poor to access many services other than through an NGO. The consequence of this 'dependent' relationship is that the poor are less likely to demand stronger accountability mechanisms as long as the services are being delivered in a fair and reasonable manner. Less than a third of the NGOs surveyed had put in place strong accountability mechanisms that saw a direct accounting of their actions or decisions to the groups they were working with. That is, few of the NGOs went beyond merely providing information on the day-to-day activities of a particular programme (a relatively low level of accountability) to seeking input from the aid recipients (the SHGs) on a range of issues with respect to the programmes. While there are no compelling programming reasons why formal accountability mechanisms should exist for agencies such as NGOs that are providing services, as a basic sharing of information would be sufficient; the research found that those NGOs with more formal mechanisms that inform the agency's strategic direction, as well as its project work, had the strongest empowerment outcomes.

The lack of demand for accountability by the aid recipients puts the NGO in the position of being able to set out the accountability relationship, unlike membership organizations such as co-operatives or unions, where the members are in some position to demand accountability, and with that have a position of power within the organization. This book argues that a voluntary reversal of the power relationship between NGOs and the people to whom they are providing services is required if high levels of empowerment are to occur. Such a reversal of power is difficult, even with the best of intentions, because handing over control can pose a potential threat to the stability and cohesion of the NGO, and make management and governance more difficult for larger NGOs. As Joshi and Moore (2000) point out, it is an exceptional NGO that is prepared to risk the basis of its work, which is about a broader public benefit, for a narrower constituent interest. Handing more power over to the recipient groups can also have the perverse effect of moving NGOs away from their original target groups, who are often more marginalized, to those who have more endowments. This latter group is in a better position to access the benefits of a particular programme if it has some control of the NGO. This paradox points to a balance needing to be found by the NGO, in which the recipient groups feel they have an influence, and therefore some power with regard to an NGO's work and direction, while the NGO maintains its public benefit purpose, adheres to its values, and expands its work to new communities if it wishes.

These findings advance the theory of community participation, which argues that the greater the level of participation of all stakeholders in programme design and implementation, particularly the beneficiaries of the activity, the greater the chance of successful outcomes for that activity. This research argues that going beyond participation, to more *formal* 'downward' accountability mechanisms is one way of NGOs (and other intermediaries) addressing the fundamental adverse power relations poor and marginalized women face in their day-to-day lives. It points to the development discourse going beyond notions of participation, with the idea of accountability as an alternative discourse, not for transparency reasons (important as they are) as much as the inherent implications for good practice in the connection of accountability to power, and empowerment processes. The challenge for NGO practice lies in how NGOs balance their accountability to the aid recipients with their accountability obligations to their values and public benefit purposes, as well as to other stakeholders in their work: the donors (the providers of resources) and governments that regulate their activities.

As we saw in Chapter 6, the issue of the accountability of NGOs to their constituency and being true to their values is a tension arising from the need to align NGO values to the priorities of the communities with which they are working. The case study NGOs from southern India all indicated that their values base did not come from the people with whom they were working as such, and they cited instances where they would not comply with the aid recipients wishes purely on the basis of conflicting values, and they have ceased programmes with some groups for these reasons. The conclusion that can be drawn is that NGOs, if they are to be intermediaries or agents for empowerment, have to establish mechanisms that recognize the power relationship they have with the people with whom they are working and be prepared to hand over some power to them. Secondly, NGOs should recognize the potential for conflicting values, and be in a position to work through such clashes in ways that empower rather than disempower the groups they are working with. While most of the NGOs in the study see themselves as empowerment agents of the poor, the analysis of both how they exercised power over, and the status they had with the communities with whom they were working, tended to compromise empowerment outcomes for most of the NGOs.

The study found that few of the case study NGOs had a sufficiently sophisticated analysis of this power relationship or empowerment processes to be able to put into place mechanisms to counter the oligarchic trends that come with being a source of resources. It also raises the question of whether the processes of empowerment can ultimately lead to the autonomy of the SHG, or whether the NGO plays a more or less permanent role in the community. This is probably not a critical issue as the NGO can offer advice and expertise, something that groups often cannot get from other services, and this type of arrangement, in which the NGO maintains some links to the groups, is often requested from the group, and becomes a service of the NGO. For example, (see Chapter 3) is even starting to charge a fee for this ongoing support; of course the problem is that this 'user pay' approach can leave the poorer groups without any ongoing support.

Role of funding agencies

Another limiting factor for effective empowerment processes was the role of the donor or resource providers. The research found that while many of the NGOs interviewed had some autonomy, there were also clear power relations between donors and NGOs, and this affected the flexibility and the opportunities for NGOs to be accountable to the communities they were working with. While some donors may seek individual or community empowerment outcomes through their support to NGOs, the accountability relationship between the donor and the NGO make this more difficult to achieve, because the source of resources has a privileged position. This is increasingly the case where the sources of funding are government agencies who contract NGO to provide services. This donor privilege arises from the more formal (often contractual) requirements that are inherent in any funding relationship, meaning the NGO is required to service the needs of the funder, at the expense of the NGO's accountability to the aid recipients. Related to donor accountability is the nature of funding relationships. Most donor and government funding is bounded by the notion of the *project*. Projects are both time-bound and seek to identify (often tangible) outcomes in advance. These two requirements of the project, in the context of empowerment, implies a de facto pre-determination of what is empowerment, and how it may be achieved, which may not accord with what the recipient sees as empowering. This brings us back to a paradox identified by Tandon (1995b: 33) that predetermining what is empowering is in itself an act of power over recipients and so is disempowering. In effect, a *project* approach instrumentalizes the notion of empowerment and so devalues it.

The implications of the findings on empowerment being identified with agency and the expansion of an individual's influence and power into new social and political domains is that these changes cannot be easily predicted, time-limited, or articulated in advance as expected outcomes. Funding bodies' resources unfortunately are usually predicated on these conditions, and as a result the expectation of the donor is privileged over the needs of the aid recipient. While the study did not look at the issue in great detail, it is worth noting that the three agencies – SNDT, IDS and Grama Vikas – that ranked highly on empowerment outcomes all had long-term, open and flexible funding relationships at the time of the field study. The donors in these three cases, while demanding detailed financial accountability, were very open to innovative, long-term processes, for which they accepted that measurable outcomes would only be realized over time. The research findings suggest a more flexible approach to funding support by agencies if empowerment is to occur. This will be difficult at a time when official donors and domestic government funders are seeking more certainty in terms of outcomes, and are promoting higher levels of control in the programme management processes, with purchaser provider contracts and the like (Kilby 2004a). Similarly, for NGOs there are aspects of their own approach programme management that can be reassessed for empowerment programmes: a focus on flexible time-frames in terms of the engagement with the communities; a clearer focus on promoting decision-making skills among group members; and most importantly a conscious focus on more formal accountability mechanisms of NGOs to the aid recipients. This flexible approach suggests handing greater control to the recipient groups which, as this book has noted, raises the new set of problems touched on earlier in this chapter. The book has also identified some innovative approaches to overcome some of these problems. An example of this innovation is SNDT, which effectively contracts its services to a representative organization of the poor, the KKPKP (waste-pickers union), but at the same time remains free to expand its work to other groups it feels it should be working with. These findings also have implications for how empowerment and poverty allevia- tion programmes are prioritized and programmed, suggesting that changes may need to be made in how certain types of programmes (such as micro-finance) are managed.

In conclusion, this book has found that empowerment is not an abstract notion, but is real in the lives of the poor and marginalized women who see it primarily in terms of agency; that is, an expansion of both their choices and their capacity to act on those choices. An important aspect of the expansion in agency, as a consequence of development interventions, is 'downward' accountability from the facilitating organization, the NGO. This finding suggests a sharper focus on the accountability of the facilitating agency to the aid recipients in development pro- gramming. This moves the theory of participation from its being important for project outcomes to one in which a more formalized relationship between the recipient and the NGO is a part of an empowering process. This has clear implications for how poverty alleviation programmes that deal with the structural causes of poverty are designed, and how development programmes and NGOs are managed. The chal- lenge that local NGOs in developing countries face is that as they become less dependent on foreign aid for poverty alleviation programmes, there will inevitably be a shift, at least in the short term, for national governments to move their funding away from empowerment programmes to more direct service delivery by NGOs. This will inevitably leave a gap in resourcing for local NGOs if they are to do innovative work. The case studies in Chapters 3 and 4 demonstrate that different and innovative resourcing models are possible and the challenge for INGO donors and others is to give them the time and space to make the transition.

References

Abbi, A. K. (1999) 'External Programme Evaluation Report of Chinyard', Tadas, Dharwad District, Karnataka: Chinyard.

AccountAble (2008) 'Charitable Purpose and Income tax', *AccountAble*, New Delhi: Feb–March.

Ackerson, B. J. and W. D. Harrison (2000) 'Practitioners' perceptions of empowerment', *Families in Society*, 81(3): 238–244.

Ahmed, S. M., Chowdhury, R., Bhuiya, A. (2001) 'Micro-credit and emotional well-being: Experience of poor rural women from Matlab, Bangladesh', *World Development*, 29(11): 1957–1966.

Anand, J. S. (2002) 'Self-help groups in empowering women: case study of selected SHGs and NHGs', Discussion Paper 38, Thiruvananthapuram: Kerala Research Programme on Local Level Development, Centre for Development Studies.

Arnstein, S. R. (1969) 'A ladder of citizen participation', *Journal of the American Institute of Planners*, 35: 216–224.

Asthana, S., 1996. 'Women's health and women's Empowerment: a locality perspective', *Health and Place*, 2(1):1–13.

Bachrach, P. and Barantz, M. S. (1970) *Power and Poverty: Theory and Practice*, London: Oxford University Press.

Banerjee, N. (2004) 'Nari Bikash Sangha: Towards Empowerment', *Indian Journal of Gender Studies*, 11: 170–203.

Baruah, B. (2007) 'Assessment of public–private–NGO partnerships: Water and sanitation services in slums', *Natural Resources Forum*, 31(3): 226–237.

Batliwala, S. (2007) 'Taking the power out of empowerment – an experiential account', *Development in Practice*, 17(4–5): 557–565.

Bava, N. (1997) 'Towards an integrated theory of people's participation through NGOs' in N. Bava, (ed.) *Non-Government Organisations in Development: Theory and Practice*, Ch 1. New Delhi: Kanishka Publications.

Baxi, U. (1997) 'Activism at the Crossroads with Signposts', in N. Bava (ed.) *Non-Government Organisations in Development: Theory and Practice*, Ch 3. New Delhi: Kanishka Publications.

Berg, C., Bredenbeck, K., Schurmann, A., Stanzick, J. and Vaneker, C. (1998) *NGO-Based Participatory Impact Monitoring of an Integrated Rural Development Project in Holalkere Taluk, Karnataka State India*, CATAD, Humboldt University, Berlin.

Bhattacharya, M. (1987) 'Voluntary associations and the state', *Indian Journal of Public Administration*, 23(3): 559–568.

Blair, H. (2000) 'Participation and accountability at the periphery: democratic governance in six countries', *World Development*, 28(1): 21–39.

Blamey, D. L. and Pasha, M. K. (1993) 'Civil society and democracy in the Third World: ambiguities and historical possibility', *Studies in Comparative International Development*, 28(1): 3–24.

Bosher, L. S., Penning-Rowsell, E., Tapsell, S. (2007) 'Resource accessibility and vulnerability in Andhra Pradesh: caste and non-caste influences', *Development and Change*, 38(4): 615–640.

Brown, J. (1974) 'Gandhi and the Indian Peasants, 1917–22', *Journal of Peasant Studies*, 1(4): 462–485.

Calman, L. J. (1992) *Towards Empowerment: Women and Movement Politics in India*, Boulder, Colorado:Westview Press.

Campbell, C. and Jovchelovitch, S. (2000) 'Health, community and development: towards a social psychology of participation', *Journal of Community and Applied Social Psychology*, 10: 255–270.

CARE (Credit Analysis and Research) (2009) 'Grading of Micro-Financing Institutions Report: Chinyard', Mumbai: CARE.

Census of India (2002) 'Provisional Results', *Census of India 2001*, Retrieved June 2002, from www.censusindia.net.

Census of India (2001) 'Sex composition of the population', *Provisional Population Totals*, New Delhi, Census of India 2001, Ch. 6.

Chandhoke, N. (1995) *State and Civil Society: explorations in political theory*, New Delhi: Sage.

Chandhoke, N. and A. Ghosh (1995) *Grassroots Movements and Social Change*, New Delhi: Developing Countries Research Centre, University of Delhi.

Chaturvedi, H. R. (1987) 'The role of voluntary organisations in rural development', *Indian Journal of Public Administration*, 23(3): 531–546.

Chazan, N. (1992) 'Africa's democratic challenge', *World Policy Journal*, 9(2): 279–307.

Cheater, A. (1999) 'Power in the postmodern era', in A. Cheater (ed.) *The Anthropology of Power*, Ch. 1. London: Routledge.

Chelliah, R. J. and Sudarshan, R. (1999) *Income Poverty and Beyond: Human Development in India*, New Delhi: UNDP.

Chikaramane, P. and Narayan, L. (2005) 'Organising the Unorganised: a Case Study of the Kagad Kach Patra Kashtakari Panchayat (Trade union of Waste-pickers)', Pune: KKPKP.

Chinyard (1999) 'Marching towards light: Chinyard Annual Report 1998–99', Agadi, Dharwad District, Karnataka: Chinyard.

Chowdry, D. P. (1987) 'Critical appraisal of voluntary effort in social welfare and development since independence', *Indian Journal of Public Administration*, 23(3): 498–503.

CIA (2008) *World Factbook*, Washington: CIA.

Conger, J. A. and Kanungo, R. N. (1988) 'The empowerment process: integrating theory and practice', *Academy of Management Review*, 1988(3): 471–482.

Cornwall, A. and Brock, K. (2005) 'What do buzzwords do for development policy? A critical look at 'participation', 'empowerment' and 'poverty reduction', *Third World Quarterly*, 26(7): 1043–1060.

Couto, R. A. (1998) 'Community coalitions and grassroots policies of empowerment', *Administration and Society*, 30(5): 569–594.

Das, M. ed. (2005) 'Karnataka Human Development Report 2005: Investing in Human Development', Bangalore: Planning and Statistics Department, Government of Karnataka.

Das, R. (2008) 'Nation, Gender and Representations of (In)Securities in Indian Politics: Secular-Modernity and Hindutva Ideology', *European Journal of Women's Studies*, 15(3): 203–221.

Datta, P. (2006) 'Urbanisation In India', European Population Conference, Liverpool: 21–24 June.

Davis, S. (1995). 'Democratisation and sustainable rural livelihoods'. *The Democratic Developmental State: Politics and Institutional Design*. M. Robinson and G. White (eds). Oxford, Oxford University Press.

Day, P. and Klein, R. (1987) *Accountabilities: Five Public Services*, London: Tavistock.

Deaton, A. and Dreze, J. (2002) 'Poverty and Inequality in India', *Economic and Political Weekly*, (Sept. 7): 3729–3748.

Desai, V. and Howes, M. (1995) 'Accountability and participation: a case study from Bombay', in M. Edwards and D. Hulme (eds). *NGO Performance and Accountability*, Ch. 8. London: Earthscan.

Dhanagare, D. N. (1990) 'Action groups and social transformation in India: some sociological issues', in C. Lakshmanna, S. P. Srivastava, and R. C. Sarikwal (eds) *Social Action and Social Change*, Ch. 8. New Delhi: Ajanta Publications.

Directorate of Economics and Statistics, (2009) 'Economic Survey of Karnataka', Bangalore: Government of Karnataka.

Drury, J. and Reicher, S. (1999) 'The intergroup dynamics of collective empowerment: substantiating the social identity model of crowd behaviour', *Group Processes and Intergroup Relations*, 2(4): 381–402.

Dutt, C. S. (2004) 'Working for women's empowerment: issues before the agency that catalyses change', *Indian Journal of Gender Studies*, 11: 156–177.

Ebrahim, A. (2001) 'NGO Behavior and Development Discourse: Cases from Western India', *Voluntas*, 12(2): 79–101.

—— (2003) *NGOs and Organizational Change*, Cambridge: Cambridge University Press.

Edwards, M. (1999a) 'Legitimacy and values in NGOs and voluntary organisations: some sceptical thoughts', in D. Lewis (ed.) *International Perspectives on Voluntary Action: Reshaping the Third Sector*, London: Earthscan.

—— (1999b) 'NGO performance – what breeds success? New evidence from South Asia', *World Development*, 27(2): 361–374.

—— (1997) 'Organisational learning in non-governmental organisations: what have we learned?', *Public Administration and Development*, 17(2): 235–250.

—— Hulme, D. (1995) 'Introduction and overview', in M. Edwards and D. Hulme (eds) *NGO Performance and Accountability*, Ch. 1. London: Earthscan.

Edwards, M. and Sen, G. (2000) 'NGOs, social change and the transformation of human relationships: a 21st century civic agenda', *Third World Quarterly*, 21(4): 605–616.

Elliot, C. (1987) 'Some aspects of relations between the north and south in the NGO Sector', *World Development*, Supplement, 15: 57–68.

Ferejohn, J. (1999) 'Accountability and authority: towards a theory of political accountability', in A. Przeworski (ed.) *Community, Accountability and Representation*, London: Cambridge University Press.

Fernandez, A. P.(1998) *The Myrada Experience: Alternate Management Systems for Savings and Credit*, Bangalore: Myrada.

—— (2001) *The Myrada Experience: Putting Institutions First – Even in Microfinance*, Bangalore: Myrada.

—— (2004) 'NGOs and Government in Collaboration for Development', *Myrada Rural Management Systems Series, Paper 39*, Bangalore: Myrada.

Filmer, D., King, E. M., Pritchett, L. (1998) *Gender disparities in South Asia: comparisons between and within countries*, Washington: World Bank.

Finn, V., Fioramonti, H., Fioramonti, L. eds (2008) *Civicus: Global survey of the State and Civil Society, Comparative Perspectives*, Bloomfield: Kumarian.

Fisher, F. (1994) 'Is the iron law of oligarchy rusting away in the Third World?', *World Development*, 22(2): 129–140.

Fowler, A. (1996) 'Strengthening civil society in transition economies – from concept to strategy: mapping an exit in a maze of mirrors', in A. Clayton (ed.) *NGOs, Civil Society and the State – Building Democracy in Transition Societies*, Oxford: INTRAC.

—— (2000a) 'NGDOs as a moment in history: beyond aid to social entrepreneurship or civic innovation', *Third World Quarterly*, 21(4): 637–654.

—— (2000b) 'Civil society NGDOs and social development: changing the rules of the game', *Occasional Paper No. 1*, Geneva: UNRISD.

Fox, J. A. and Brown, D. L. eds (1998) *The Struggle for Accountability: The World Bank, NGOs and Grassroots Movements*, Cambridge Massachusetts: MIT Press.

Gaiha, R. and K. Imai (2004) 'Vulnerability, shocks and persistence of poverty: estimates for semi-arid rural South India', *Oxford Development Studies*, 32(2): 261–281.

Gerard, D. (1983) *Charities in Britain: Conservatism of change?*, London: Bedford Square Press.

Giddens, A. (1979) *Central Problems in Social Theory: Action, Structure, and Contradictions in Social Analysis*, London: MacMillan.

—— (1984) *The Constitution of Society: Outline of the Theory of Structuration*, Cambridge: Polity Press.

Grama Vikas (2000) 'From subsistence to substance', mimeo, Grama Vikas, Honnsetthalli, Kolar District, Karnataka.

Goetz, Anne-Maire (2006) 'Gender and Accountability: Challenges for Reform in Developing States', The Boston Consortium on Gender, Security and Human Rights, Boston: Fletcher School of Law and Diplomacy, Tufts University, 10 April.

—— (2001) *Women Development Workers: Implementing Rural Credit Programs in Bangladesh*, New Delhi: Sage.

Goetz, A-M. and Gupta, R. S. (1996) 'Who takes credit? Gender, power, and control over loan use in rural credit program in Bangladesh', *World Development*, 24(1): 45–63.

Gorain, S. (1993) 'Training grassroots level workers in empowering the rural poor: the case of an Indian NGO', *The Indian Journal of Social Work*, 54(3): 381–392.

Gray, R., Dey, C., Owen, D., Evans, R. and Zadek, S. (1997) 'Struggling with the praxis of social accounting: stakeholders, accountability, audits and procedures', *Accounting, Auditing and Accountability Journal* , 10 (3): 325–364.

Hall, A. L. and Rist, R. C. (1999) 'Integrating multiple qualitative research methods (or avoiding the precariousness of a one-legged stool)', *Psychology and Marketing*, 16(4): 291–304.

Handy, F. and Kasam, M. (2006) 'Practice What You Preach? The Role of Rural NGOs in Women's Empowerment', *Journal of Community Practice* , 14(3): 69–91.

Hashemi, S. M., Schuler, S. R., Riley, A. P. (1996) 'Rural credit programs and women's empowerment in Bangladesh', *World Development*, 24(4): 635–653.

Hilemath, S. ed. (2004) 'IDS Evolution: lessons learnt', India Development Service Dharwad, Silver Jubilee Year 2003–2004 Souvenir, Dharwad: IDS.

Hindess, B. (1996) *Discourses of Power: From Hobbes to Foucault*, Oxford: Blackwell.

Hines, A. M. (1993) 'Linking qualitative and quantitative methods in cross-cultural research: techniques from cognitive science', *American Journal of Community Psychology*, 21(3): 729–746.

Hirschman, D. (1998) 'Civil society in South Africa: learning from gender themes', *World Development*, 26(2): 227–238.

Hishigsuren (2000) 'Holistic Approaches to Development: Practitioner-led impact assessment of ASA', Tiruchirapalli, India: ASA.

Hollander, E. P. and Offermann, L. R. (1990) 'Power and leadership in organizations: relationships in transition', *American Psychologist*, 45: 179–189.

Howes, M. (1997) 'NGOs and the institutional development of membership organisations: the evidence from six case studies', *Journal of International Development*, 9(4): 597–604.

Imandar, N. R. (1987) 'Role of voluntarism in development', *Indian Journal of Public Administration*, 23(3): 421–430.

Isern, J., Prakash, L. B., Pillai, A., Hashemi, S., Christen, R. P., Ivatury, G. I., Rosenberg, R. (2007) 'Sustainability of Self-Help Groups in India: Two Analyses', Occasional Paper No. 12, Washington: Consultative Group to Assist the Poor (CGAP).

Iyengar, S. (2000) 'Role of Non-Governmental Organisations in the development of Gujarat', *Economic and Political Weekly*, (Aug 26–Sept 2).

Jain, R. B. (1997) 'NGOs in India: their role, influence and problems', in N. Bava *Non-Government Organisations in Development: Theory and Practice*, New Delhi: Kanishka Publications.

Jalali, R. (2008) 'International Funding of NGOs in India: Bringing the State Back In', *Voluntas*, 19: 161–188.

Janardhan, N. (1995) 'Lesson from a women's development project: do poor women have a choice?' *Asia-Pacific Development Journal*, 2(2): 37–49.

Jandhyala, K. (1998) 'Women, empowerment and the state', *The Indian Journal of Social Work*, 59(1): 191–208.

Jenkins, R. (1998) 'The Development Implications of Federal and Political Institutions in India', in M. Robinson and G. White (eds) *The Democratic Developmental State: Politics and Institutional Design*, Oxford: Oxford University Press.

Jenkins, R. and Goetz, A-M. (1999) 'Accounts and accountability: theoretical implications of the right-to-information movement in India', *Third World Quarterly*, 20(3): 603–622.

Jha, R. (2002) 'Reducing Poverty and Inequality in India: Has Liberalization Helped?', Departmental Working Papers, Canberra: Australian National University, Economics RSPAS.

Jordan, L. (2005) 'Mechanisms for NGO accountability', *GPPi Research Paper Series*, Global Public Policy Institute, No. 3.

Joseph, H. (1997) 'Social work with groups: a literature review', *The Indian Journal of Social Work*, 58(2): 195–211.

Joshi, A. and Moore, M. (2000) 'Enabling environments: do anti-poverty programmes mobilise the poor?', *The Journal of Development Studies*, 37(1): 25–56.

Joshi, S. (2003) 'Decent proposal: NGOs welcome draft policy on voluntary sector', *Down To Earth: Science and Environment Journal*, 12: 13.

Kabeer, N. (1999) 'Resources, agency, achievements: reflections on measures of women's empowerment', *Development and Change*, 30(3): 435–464.

—— (2001) 'Conflicts over credit: re-evaluating the empowerment potential of loans to women in rural Bangladesh', *World Development*, 29(1): 63–84.

—— (2005) 'Gender Equality and Women's Empowerment: A Critical Analysis of the Third Millennium Development Goal', *Gender and Development*, 13(1): 13–24.

Kane, K. and Montgomery, K. (1998) 'A framework for understanding dysempowering organisations', *Human Resource Management*, 37(3&4): 263–275.

Kantor, P. (2003) 'Women's empowerment through home-based work: evidence from India', *Development and Change*, 34(3): 425–445.

Karlekar, M. (2004) 'A note on the empowerment of women', *Indian Journal of Gender Studies*, 11(2): 145–155.

Kaushik, S. (1997) 'NGOs and development: some issues', in N. Bava (ed.) *Non-Government Organisations in Development: Theory and Practice*, New Delhi: Kanishka Publications.

KIDS (2000a) 'Annual Report 1999–2000', Dharwad, Karnataka: KIDS.

—— (2000b) *Manavi: a commitment of women and children*, Dharwad, Karnataka: KIDS.

Kilby, P. (2004) 'Non-Governmental Organisations in an era of Global Anxiety', *Seton Hall Journal of Diplomacy and International Relations*, 5(2): 67–78.

—— (2004a) 'Is Empowerment Possible under a New Public Management Environment? some lessons from India', *International Public Management Journal*, 7(2): 207–225.

—— (2006) 'Accountability for empowerment: dilemmas facing non governmental organizations', *World Development*, 34(6): 951–963.

Kothari, R. (1987) 'Voluntary organisations in a plural society', *Indian Journal of Public Administration*, 23(5): 559–568.

Krishna, A. (2006) 'Pathways out of and into poverty in 36 villages of Andhra Pradesh, India', *World Development*, 34(2): 271–288.

Kudva, N. (2005) 'Strong States, Strong NGOs', in R. Ray and M. F. Katzenstein (eds) *Social Movements in India: poverty, power, and politics*, Ch. 9. Lanham: Rowan and Littlefield.

—— (2008) 'Conceptualising NGO-State Relations in Karnataka: Conflict and Collaboration Amidst Organisational Diversity', in G. K. Kadekodi, R. Kanbur and V. Rao (eds) *Developments in Karnataka: Challenges of Governance, Equity and Empowerment*, Ch. 6. New Delhi: Academic Foundation.

Kumar, R. (1969) 'Class, Community or Nation? Gandhi's Quest for political Consensus in India', *Modern Asian Studies*, 3(4): 357–376.

Lee, H., Herr, P. M., Kordes, I. R. and Kim, C. 1999. 'Motivated search: effect of choice accountability, issue involvement and prior knowledge in information acquisition and use', *Journal of Business Research*, 45: 75–88.

Lingam, L. (1998) 'Taking stocks: women's movement and the state', *The Indian Journal of Social Work*, 59(1): 167–190.

Lissner, J. (1977) *The Politics of Altruism: A Study of the Political Behaviours of Voluntary Development Agencies*, Geneva: Lutheran World Federation.

Loughhead, S., Mittal, O., Wood, G. (2001) 'Urban Poverty and Vulnerability in India: DFID's Experiences from a Social Policy Perspective', London: DFID.

Lukes, S. (1974) *Power: A Radical View*, London: Macmillan.

Madriz, E. L. (1998) 'Using focus groups with lower socioeconomic status – latina women', *Qualitative Inquiry*, 4(1):114–128.

Makeshwari, R. (1987) 'Voluntary action in rural development in India', *Indian Journal of Public Administration*, 23(3): 559–568.

Mander, H. (2002) 'Savaged by tradition', *Frontline*, 19(24) November 23 – December 6.

Markham, W. T. and Bonjean, C. M. (1995) 'Community orientations of higher status women volunteers', *Social Forces*, 73(4): 1553–1571.

Maxwell, D., Webb, P., Coates, J., Wirth, J. (2008). 'Rethinking Food Security in Humanitarian Response', Food Security Forum April 16–18. Rome Tufts University, Friedman School of Nutrition Science and Policy, and Feinstein International Center.

Mayoux, L. (1999) 'Questioning virtuous spirals: micro-finance and women's empowerment in Africa', *Journal of International Development*, 11: 957–984.

—— (2000) *'Micro-finance and the empowerment of women – A review of the key issues' paper for International Labour Organization (ILO)*, Geneva: ILO.

—— (2001) 'Tackling the down side: social capital, women's empowerment and micro-finance in Cameroon', *Development and Change*, 32(3): 421–450.

McDonald, C. (1999) 'Internal control and accountability in non-profit human service organisations', *Australian Journal of Public Administration*, 58(1): 11–22.

Meenakshi, J. V. and R. Ray (2003) 'How Have the Disadvantaged Fared in India? An Analysis of Poverty and Inequality in the 1990s', in K. Sharma (ed.) *Trade Policy, Growth, and Poverty in Asian Developing Countries*, Ch. 12. New York: Routledge.

Mehta, A. K. and A. Shah (2003) 'Chronic Poverty in India: Incidence, Causes and Policies', *World Development*, 31(3): 491–511.

Milne, G. (2007) 'Karnataka Watershed Development "Sujala" Project: Innovation in participatory watershed development to improve natural resource productivity and rural livelihoods', in S. S. Banerjee (ed) *Livelihoods Learning Series 1, Note No. 3*. Washington: World Bank.

Ministry of Home Affairs (2007) *FCRA Annual Report*, New Delhi: Government of India.

Ministry of Home Affairs (2008) 'FCRA for NGOs', at http://fcraforngos.org (accessed July 2008).

Ministry of Social Justice and Empowerment (2004) *Annual Report 2003–2004*, New Delhi: Government of India.

Mishra, D., Biswas, S. N., Roy, S. (2006) 'Governance of NGOS: contextualizing in the Indian experience', *International Journal of Rural Management I*, 1(2): 185–201.

Mohanty, M. and A. K. Singh (2001) *Voluntarism and Government: Policy, Programme and Assistance*, New Delhi: Voluntary Action Network India (VANI).

Moore, M. (2001) 'Empowerment at last?' *Journal of International Development*, 13: 321–329.

Moyle, T. L., Dollard, M, Biswas, S. N. (2006) 'Personal and economic empowerment in rural Indian women: a self-help group approach', *International Journal of Rural Management*, 2: 245–266.

Mulgan, R. (2001) 'The accountability of community sector agencies: a comparative framework', Discussion paper No. 85, Graduate Program in Public Policy, Canberra: Asia Pacific School of Economics and Government, ANU.

Murgai, R., Suryanarayana, M. H., and Zaidi, S. (2003) 'Measuring Poverty in Karnataka: the regional dimension', *Economic and Political Weekly*, Jan 25: 404–408.

Murthi, M., Guio, A., Dreze, J. (1996) 'Mortality and Fertility in Gender Bias in India: a district level analysis', in D. J. and A. Sen. (eds) *Indian Development: Selected Regional Perspectives*, Ch.1. New Delhi: Oxford University Press.

Murthy, R. K. (2001) 'Introduction', in R. K. Murthy(ed.) *Building Women's Capacities: Interventions in Gender Transformations*, Ch. 1. New Delhi: Sage.

—— (2004) 'Organisational strategy in India and diverse identities of women: bridging the gap', *Gender and Development*, 12(1): 10–18.

Murthy, R. K. and Rao, N. (1997) *Addressing Poverty: Indian NGOs and Their Capacity Enhancement in the 1990s*, New Delhi: Friedrich Ebart Stiftung.

Myrada (2009) 'Annual Report 2008–2009', Bangalore: Myrada.

Nagar, R. and Raju, S. (2003) 'Women, NGOs and the Contradictions of Empowerment and Disempowerment: A Conversation', *Antipode*: 1–13.

Nanavatty, M. C. (1987) 'Role of central social welfare board in the changing social context', *Indian Journal of Public Administration*, 23(3): 501–511.

Nandedkar, V. G. (1987) 'Voluntary associations: a strategy for development', *Indian Journal of Public Administration*, 23(3): 460–480.

Narayan, D. (1999) *Can anyone hear us? Voices from 47 countries*, Washington, D. C.: The World Bank Poverty Group, PREM.

Nayar, K., Kyobutungi, R. C., Razum, O. (2004) 'Self-help: What future role in health care for low and middle-income countries?' *International Journal for Equity in Health*, 3(1): 1.

Ninan, K. N. (2000) 'Economic reforms in India: impact on the poor and poverty reduction' Working Paper 102, Brighton: Institute of Development Studies.

Padaki, V. (2000) 'Coming to grips with Organisational Values', *Development in Practice*, 10(3/4): 420–435.

Panagariya, A. (2004) 'India in the 1980s and 1990s: A Triumph of Reforms' IMF Working Paper (WP/04/43) Washington: International Monetary Fund.

Pantoja, E. (1999) 'Exploring the Concept of Social Capital and its Relevance for Community-based Development: The Case of Mining areas in Orissa, India', Draft Paper, Social Capital Initiative, South Asia Infrastructure Unit, Washington: The World Bank.

Parker, B., Kozel, Kukreja M. (2003) 'In search of a chance: Urban opportunities, poverty and vulnerability in Uttar Pradesh, India', paper presented at World Bank Urban Research Symposium Dec 15–17. Washington: World Bank.

Parker, P. (2007) 'PRS Legislative Brief on Foreign Contributions Regulations Bill: Sarkar-approved contributions only', *India Together*, www.indiatogether.org/2007/mar/law-fcrbill. htm, accessed June 9, 2008.

Paton, R. (1993) 'The social economy: value-based organizations in the wider society', in J. Batsleer, C. Cornforth and R. Paton (eds) *Issues in Voluntary and Non-profit Management*, Wokingham: Addison-Wesley: 3–12.

Peters, B. G. and Pierre, J. (2000) 'Citizen versus the new public manager', *Administration and Society*, 32(1): 9–28.

Pilsuk, M., McAllister, J., Rothman, R. (1996) 'Coming together for action: the challenges of contemporary grassroots community organising', *Journal of Social Issues*, 52(1): 15–37.

Planning Commission (2007) 'National Policy on the Voluntary Sector', New Delhi: Voluntary Action Cell, Planning Commission of India, Government of India.

Planning Commission (2007a) 'Poverty Estimates for 2004–2005', New Delhi: Planning Commission of India, Government of India.

Poland, B. and Pederson, A. (1998) 'Reading between the lines: interpreting silences in qualitative research', *Qualitative Inquiry*, 4(2): 293–312.

Power, G., Maury, M., Maury, S. (2002) 'Operationalising bottom-up learning in international NGOs: barriers and alternatives', *Development in Practice*, 12(3&4): 272–284.

Prakruthi (n.d.) 'Organisational Profile of Prakruthi' Seegenahalli, Karnataka: Prakruthi.

Premi, M. K. (2002) 'Progress of Literacy in India: what the census of 2001 Reveals', NIEPA Seminar India's Literacy Panorama; New Delhi: October 5.

PRIA (2009) 'An Analysis of the Constraints and Challenges in the Utilisation of the Scheduled Caste Sub Plan' New Delhi: PRIA.

Puroshothaman, S. (1998) *The Empowerment of Women in India: Grassroots Women's Network and the State*, New Delhi: Sage.

Rahman, A. (1999) 'Micro-credit initiatives for equitable and sustainable development: who pays?' *World Development*, 27(1): 67–82.

Rajasekhar, D. (1998) 'Rural Development Strategies of NGOs', *Journal of Social and Economic Development*, 1(2): 306–327.

Rajasekhar, D. (2000) 'Non-Governmental Organisations (NGOs) in India: Opportunities and Challenges', *Journal of Rural Development*, 19(2): 249–275.

Reddy, I. (1987) 'Role of voluntary agencies in development', *Indian Journal of Public Administration*, 23(3): 547–558.

Reid, P. T. and Vianna, E. (2001) 'Negotiating partnership in research on poverty with community-based agencies', *Journal of Social Issues*, 57(2): 337–354.

Riger, S. (1993) 'What's wrong with empowerment?' *American Journal of Community Psychology*, 21(3): 279–292.

Robinson-Pant, A. (2004) 'The Illiterate Woman: changing approaches to researching women's literacy', in A. Robinson-Pant (ed.) *Women, literacy, and development: alternative perspectives*, Ch. 1. Oxford: Routledge.

Robinson, M. (1995) 'Democracy, participation and public policy: the politics of institutional design', in M. Robinson and G. White (eds) *The Democratic Developmental State: Politics and Institutional Design*, Ch. 5. Oxford: Oxford University Press.

Rose, R. (1980) 'The Nature of the challenge', in R. Rose (ed.) *Challenge to Governance: Studies in Overloaded Politics*, Ch. 1. London: Sage Publications.

Sabatini, C. A. (2002) 'Whom do international donors support in the name of civil society?' *Development in Practice*, 12(1): 7–19.

Salamon, L. M. and Anheier, H. K. (1997) *Defining the non-profit sector: a cross-national analysis*, Manchester: Manchester University Press.

—— (1999) 'The Third World's third sector comparative advantage' in D. Lewis (ed.) *International Perspectives on Voluntary Action: Reshaping the Third Sector*, Ch. 3. London: Earthscan.

Samson, M. ed. (2009) *Refusing to be Cast Aside: waste-pickers organising around the world*, Cambridge MA: Women in Informal Employment: Globalising and Organising (WIEGO).

Sandelowski, M. (2000) 'Combining qualitative and quantitative sampling: data collection, and analysis techniques in mixed method studies', *Research in Nursing and Health*, 23: 246–255.

Schneider, H. (1999) 'Participatory governance for poverty reduction', *Journal of International Development*, 11: 521–534.

Scurrah, M. J. (1996) 'NGOs, civil society and democracy in Peru: idea and experiences', in A. Clayton (ed.) *NGOs, Civil Society and the State – Building Democracy in Transition Societies* Ch. 5, Oxford: INTRAC.

Seibel, W. (1990) 'Organisational behaviour and organisational function: towards a micro-macro theory of the third sector', H. K. Anheier and W. Seibel (eds) *The Third Sector Comparative Studies of Non profit Organisations*, Berlin: Walter de Gruyter.

Sen, A. (1999) *Development as Freedom*, New York: Alfred A Knopf.

Sen, G. (1997) 'Empowerment as an Approach to Poverty', Working Paper Series, Global Reproductive Health Forum.

Sen, S. (1992) 'Non-profit organisations in India: historical perspectives and common patterns', *Voluntas*, 3(2): 175–193.

—— (1997) 'India' in L. M. Salamon and H. K. Anheier (eds) *Defining the Non-profit Sector: A Cross-national Analysis*, Manchester: Manchester University Press: 401–445.

—— (1999) 'Some aspects of state NGO relationships in India in the post-independence era', *Development and Change*, 30(2): 327–355.

—— (1993) 'Defining the Nonprofit Sector: India' in L. M. Salamon and H. K. Anheier (eds) *The Johns Hopkins Comparative Nonprofit Sector Project*, Baltimore: Maryland, USA, Morgan State University.

Sen, S. and Mukherjee, I. (2006) 'The Changing Status of Women in India – the Challenges Ahead, *SSRN*, available at SSRN: http://ssrn.com/abstract=920326. (accessed Aug 2008).

Seth, D. L. and Sethi, H. (1991) 'The NGO sector in India: historical context and current discourse', *Voluntas*, 2(2): 44–68.

Sharma, A. (2006) 'Crossbreeding Institutions, Breeding Struggle: Women's Empowerment, Neoliberal Governmentality, and State (Re)Formation in India', *Cultural Anthropology*, 21(1): 60–95.

Schedler, A. (1999) 'Power and Accountability' in A. Schedler, L. Diamond, and M. F Platner (eds) *New Democracies*, London: Lynne Rienner: 13–28.

Sheth, N. R. (1996) 'A perspective for the sociology of Indian organisations', in A. M. Shah, B. S. Barishar and E. A. Ramaswamy (eds) *Social Structure and Change: Complex Organisations and Urban Communities*, New Delhi: Sage.

Siddiqui, H. Y. (1997) 'Analysis of literature of social action', *The Indian Journal of Social Work*, 58(2): 212–232.

Slim, H. (1997) 'Relief agencies and moral standing in war – principles of humanity, neutrality, impartiality and solidarity', *Development in Practice*, 7(4): 342–352.

Smith-Sreen, P. (1995) *Accountability in Development Organisations: Experiences of Women's Organisations in India*, New Delhi: Sage.

Speer, P. W. (2000) 'Intrapersonal and interactional empowerment: implications for theory', *Journal of Community Psychology*, 28(1): 51–61.

Spodek, H. (1971) 'On the Origins of the Gandhi's Political Methodology: The Heritage of Kathiawad and Gujarat' *The Journal of Asian Studies*, 30(2): 361–372.

Srinivasan, B. (2007) 'In the Crucible: When development, poverty and fundamentalism combine', *Development*, 50: 122–126.

Syed, H. and M. Hassan (1999) 'Building NGO legitimacy in Bangladesh: the contested domain' in D. Lewis (ed) *International Perspectives on Voluntary Action; Reshaping the Third Sector*, Ch. 6. London: Earthscan.

Tandon, R. (1995a) 'Board games: governance and accountability', in M. Edwards and D. Hulme (eds) *NGO Performance and Accountability*, Ch. 3. London: Earthscan.

—— (1995b) 'Poverty, process of impoverishment and empowerment', in V. Titi and N. Singh (eds) *Empowerment for Sustainable Development: Towards Operational Strategies*, Ch. 2. Nova Scotia: Zed Books.

—— (2002) 'Address by Dr. Rajesh Tandon from Voluntary Sector' All India Conference on the Role of the Voluntary Sector in National Development, 20th April, Vigyan Bhavan, New Delhi.

Tata Energy Research Institute (2001) 'Karnataka Watershed Development Project: Report on Regional Environmental Assessment And Social Assessment' Karnataka Watershed Development Project, Bangalore: Watershed Development Department Government of Karnataka.

Tayler, K. (2005) 'An Institutional approach to service-provision partnerships in South Asia', *Development in Practice*, 15(3): 337–348.

Tesoriero, F. (2005) 'Strengthening communities through women's self help groups in South India', *Community Development Journal*, 41(3): 321–333.

Thorp, R., Stewart, F. et al. (2005) 'When and how far is group formation a route out of chronic poverty?', *World Development* 33(6): 907–920.

Thorp, R., Stewart, F., Heyer, A. (2005) 'When and how far is group formation a route out of chronic poverty?' *World Development*, 33(6): 907–920.

Times of India (2003) 'India's makeover: From aid-taking to aid-giving', *Times of India, June 2*: New Delhi.

Titi, V. and Singh, N. eds (1995) *Empowerment for Sustainable Development: Towards Operational Strategies*, Nova Scotia: Zed Books.

Townsend, J. and Townsend, A. R. (2004) 'Accountability, motivation and practice: NGOs North and South', *Social and Cultural Geography*, 5(2): 271–284.

Trivedy, R. and Acharya, J. (1996) 'Constructing a case for an alternative framework for understanding civil society, the state and the role of NGOs', in A. Clayton (ed.) *NGOs, Civil Society and the State – Building Democracy in Transition Societies*, Ch. 5. Oxford: INTRAC.

UNDP (2008) 'India: The Human Development Index – going beyond income', *Human Development Report*, New York: UNDP.

Vijayalakshmi, V. (2001) 'Politics of inclusion: scheduled tribe women in local governance', ISEC Working Paper no 88, Bangalore: ISEC.

Viswanath, V. (1993) *NGOs and Women's Development in Rural India: A Comparative Analysis*, New Delhi: Vistaar Publications.

Webler, T., and Tuler, S. (2000) 'Fairness and competence in citizen participation: theoretical reflections from a case study', *Administration and Society*, 32(5): 566–595.

Williamson, S. (1991) 'On the fringe of capitalism: the role and nature of NGOs', Master of Arts thesis, Adelaide: Flinders University.

Wiserearth. (2005) 'Chinyard Organisation Profile', Retrieved January 26, 2009, from www.wiserearth.org/organization.

Wonink, S. J., Kok, M.T. J., Hilderink, H.B. M. (2005). Vulnerability and Human Well-being Report of a workshop in preparation of Global Environment Outlook 4 – Report 500019003/2005. *Netherlands-Environmental-Assessment-Agency-(MNP-RIVN). Bilthoven.*

World Bank (2009) 'Implementation Completion and Results Report No: ICR00001205: Karnataka Watershed Development', Washington D.C: Sustainable Development Department, Agriculture and Rural Development Unit, South Asia Region, World Bank.

—— (1996) *Participation Sourcebook*, Washington, D. C: World Bank.

Zaidi, S. A. (1999) 'NGO failure and the need to bring back the state', *Journal of International Development*, 11(2): 259–271.

Zaman, H. (1999) *Assessing the Impact of Micro-credit on Poverty and Vulnerability in Bangladesh: A Case Study of BRAC*, Washington, D. C: The World Bank.

Zimmerman, M. A. and Rappaport, J. (1988) 'Citizen participation, perceived control, and psychological empowerment', *American Journal of Community Psychology*, 16: 725–750.

Index